THINGS TO DO
WHEN YOU TURN 30

Sellers Publishing, Inc.
161 John Roberts Road, South Portland, Maine 04106
Visit our Web site: www.sellerspublishing.com • E-mail: rsp@rsvp.com

Ronnie Sellers: President and Publisher
Robin Haywood: Publishing Director
Mary Baldwin: Managing Editor
Charlotte Cromwell: Production Editor
Design by: Faceout Studio

ISBN 13: 978-1-4162-0515-9
Library of Congress Control Number: 2008923446

Printed in the United States of America.

Credits: Page 248

THIRTY ACHIEVERS ON TURNING THIRTY

THINGS TO DO
WHEN YOU TURN 30

Edited by Ronnie Sellers

Commissioning Editor Chris Taylor

SELLERS
PUBLISHING

CONTENTS

SECTION ONE
Give Back to the World

SECTION TWO
Pursue Your Passion and Purpose

SECTION THREE
Get in Touch with Who You Really Are

SECTION FOUR
Nurture Your Body, Mind and Spirit

SECTION FIVE
Stretch Your Horizons

INTRODUCTION

If you are reading this, then you have reached the age where people twenty-nine and under will no longer trust you. You probably won't realize it, but they will be listening to you with a touch of skepticism. What you consider to be a friendly verbal exchange they will hear as a lecture. Their behavior will be guarded when in your presence because, whether you like it or not, you are now a part of the establishment in their eyes. Congratulations. You have reached the BIG 3-0!

You've got a couple of milestone birthdays under your belt already. Your sixteenth was okay, but you were probably a little too tied up in knots from teen angst to really appreciate it. You're twenty-first was definitely more fun than your sixteenth, at least up until the point where you downed that one last jello shot, after which your knees buckled and your eyeballs rolled up into your head.

But if you're like most people, neither of these earlier milestones did much to prepare you for turning thirty. This birthday is the real deal, the first real waypoint on the road to . . . gulp . . . maturity.

It would be disingenuous of me not to admit that I turned thirty so long ago I can't even remember what I did to mark the occasion. I intended to make an earnest effort to recall my experience before picking up the pen to write this introduction, but then I realized that I didn't know where I'd left the pen. Even worse, I couldn't remember where I'd put the damned eyeglasses I'd need to find the pen! "Who are you kidding?" I said to myself. "It's good enough that you remember where you live. Forget about remembering your thirtieth birthday!"

Besides, I'm not sure how relevant my experience would be to yours even if I could remember it. Certainly, there are things that happen during our first thirty years that are common to all of us. We all struggle to educate and prepare ourselves for a vocation. We have some successes and a few failures. We all experience rejection of one sort or another and, hopefully, find acceptance once we begin to get a stronger sense of where it is we belong. We fall in (and, often, out of) love. Many of us start families. Some of us see our families break apart. We lose people we care a great deal about.

But a lot has changed over the years as well. What has changed the most is the speed of life. As a soon-to-be thirty-year-old, you have grown up in the digital age. By the time you were ten years old you were probably as proficient with technology as the most tech-savvy members of the generation that preceded you. Now you've done them one better. They were wired. You are wireless. I'll bet that you regularly send text messages on your cell phone while surfing the Web on your laptop and listening to music on your MP3 player. You are always open for business. This has altered the way you and your contemporaries work and live.

I'll give you an example: I had lunch recently with a young man who was about to turn thirty who worked in the financial industry. As we were being escorted to our table, his PDA chimed. He removed the device from his sport coat pocket, looked at the screen, and said apologetically, "I just got an e-mail from my boss. He needs me to send him an analysis of the portfolio of one of our largest clients within an hour."

"That sounds pretty important," I said. "I will understand if you need to cancel our lunch and run back to your office."

He looked slightly surprised that I would even suggest that he should skip lunch. "No no no," he exclaimed with a wave of his hand, "that's really not necessary. I've got it covered. Just excuse me for a second while I search for the data."

I watched as his thumbs flew back and forth across the buttons on his handheld device. Seconds later he looked up at me. "Got it, it's downloading. By the way, the crab cake appetizer they have here is really awesome!" Before we'd finished eating, he had run a second report to sort the data and format it the way his boss likes to see it. Then, before the ink was dry on my credit card invoice, he e-mailed the finished analysis to his boss.

As we were heading for the restaurant exit, I asked him, "How do you feel about turning thirty?"

He stopped walking, turned to face me, and looked me squarely in the eyes. "You know, I really can't answer that question," he said somewhat ashamedly. A cloud of worry suddenly seemed to sweep over him. "I'm always so busy that I can't seem to find time to think about it."

If you are turning thirty you are probably, like the young man I had lunch with that day, a master multitasker. The more the technology evolves, the more tasks you are able to complete within a given interval of time. You have learned to utilize your time so efficiently that there is almost no limit to how much you can accomplish. And therein lies the rub. You have reached the point of ultimate efficiency for a multitasker, which is the point at which you have absolutely no extra time! Whether this is making you happy or not is a moot point because you don't have time to contemplate happiness. To do that, you'd have to log out and go offline, and that's definitely not happening.

Is this the way life is supposed to be lived? Have we replaced, "I think, therefore I am," with "I'm online, therefore I am"? Did our ancestors begin inventing tools thousands of years ago so they could do ever-increasing amounts of work? Or by inventing tools did they hope to get their work done faster so they could relax or pursue other interests, such as pondering the more esoteric aspects of life? Is fast always better than slow? Is more always better than less? Are our ingenious devices making us any happier? What is the relationship between abundance and contentment?

These conundrums are not unique to the age of the wireless World Wide Web. They have existed for as long as there has been innovation. The members of every generation have had to come to grips with the changes imposed by emerging technologies, and they had to decide the extent to which they wanted the latest and greatest widgets to alter their lives.

I've mentioned my young friend who used his handheld computer to create a financial analysis while eating lunch. Well, let me wind the clock back about fifty years and give you an example of someone who made a different choice about using technology.

I grew up within the context of a family business. My grandfather, who was raised on a farm in western North Carolina and had no formal education beyond the eighth grade, started a retail piano business in Philadelphia in the 1930s that became quite successful. My father assumed control of the business in 1960 and expanded it. He also modernized it. One of the improvements he made was to install multilined telephones. These were phone sets with a line of push buttons across the bottom and a red hold button on the left. When a call came in on a line, the button blinked. You picked up the receiver, pushed the blinking button, and spoke to the caller. If another call came in while you were talking to the first caller, you asked the first caller to "please hold," you pushed the hold button, and then you depressed the button for the second line and spoke to the second caller.

My grandfather, who was really the consummate entrepreneur in so many ways (most of which I didn't come to appreciate until I became an entrepreneur myself years later), refused to learn how to use the multilined telephones.

I will never forget how much this frustrated my father. In an attempt to relieve the tension between them regarding the telephones, I took my grandfather aside one afternoon and offered to teach him how to work the buttons on the telephone. "It's really pretty simple," I told him a bit condescendingly. "I could probably teach you how to do it in five minutes."

"Sonny boy," he said to me, "come to my office for a minute." I followed him to his office and he closed the door behind me. "I want to tell you something that you probably won't understand for many years to come," he said gently. "Over the course of my lifetime, I've seen many things change. I rode a horse to school when I was a boy. Our farmhouse had no plumbing, heating, or electricity. Life was hard. The first telephone I ever saw was in Chicago when I was seventeen years old. I love modern conveniences as much as the next person. But with each new invention, we each have to decide whether or not we want to pay the price associated with using it, and I'm not talking about the price of gas or a phone call here."

"I'm not following you," I admitted. "What price are you talking about?"

"Whenever something is gained, something is lost," he explained. "In the case of the multilined telephone, it would enable me to take calls from six different customers simultaneously. The problem is that I wouldn't be able to concentrate enough to have a decent conversation with any of them. My ability to listen and share would be compromised, and that's a price I'm not willing to pay. So I won't.

"There will be more changes coming, that's for sure," he went on to say. "Someday, these new-fangled phones with the hold buttons will seem as antiquated as the old ones we had to hand-crank before using. Just remember that none of these gadgets comes without a price. I expect you to take the time to figure out what that price is. Once you've done that, then go ahead and decide whether you want to pay it or not."

What is the price that my grandfather was referring to, and do we really have a choice about whether we want to pay it or not? I have my own opinions, but I am not someone who is turning thirty, and I am definitely not someone who can send text messages while I surf the Web and listen to music on an iPod. So I will disqualify myself.

And I will disqualify myself happily, because I have read the essays that the thirtysomething celebrities, authors, athletes, pundits, financial wizards, and health experts were kind enough to contribute for this book. They have written eloquently, and often very humorously, about their experiences of turning thirty in an era that abhors away messages and has produced twenty-three-year-old billionaires as well as cell phones that enable your every movement to be tracked by satellite.

These authors have pondered, and written, about the messes, stresses, and successes they experienced during their first thirty years. They have attempted to answer the very same question my grandfather posed to me so many years ago: what is the price of all of this ingenious innovation, and is it worth what we're paying for it? They offer concrete advice about things you can do to be healthier, happier, and possibly wealthier during the next phase of your life. They advocate reaching outside of yourself to give something back to the world.

Collectively, these essays offer a wonderfully diverse and comprehensive guide to turning thirty, a guide that will help to make the process as meaningful, enjoyable, profitable, healthy . . . and fun as possible.

So, whether you're reading this on a printed page, a computer screen, an electronic book, or listening to an audio-book version on an iPod, please sit back and enjoy the gift your contemporaries have so generously offered you as you pass this important milestone. I assure you that it will leave you feeling a little bit wiser, a little bit lighter, and a lot more hopeful about what lies ahead.

Happy 30th!
Ronnie Sellers

Section

GIVE BACK TO THE WORLD

Scratch the Itch

For this creative entrepreneur and co-founder of *mental_floss*, a trip to India brought an unexpected encounter — and a new way of thinking about giving back to the world.

by Mangesh Hattikudur

Mangesh Hattikudur is co-founder of the award-winning independent magazine *mental_floss*. His work has been featured in *Newsweek, India Today, CNN.com, Washington Post,* and *Entertainment Weekly,* and he was named to *Inc.* magazine's "30 Under 30" list of American entrepreneurs. Aside from his work on the magazine, Hattikudur has helped mental_floss produce seven books and a board game, Law School in a Box. He currently spends most of his time editing the brand's web presence at mentalfloss.com.

THEN

When I was in third grade, my friends already knew everything there was to know about India, and they told me so on the playground. Many of them had spent their summer vacations basking in the warm glow of their TV sets.

Much to my dismay, however, this was also the year that the Christian Children's Fund began airing their gritty, black-and-white commercials. The spots were clearly for a good cause, since they were encouraging Americans to share their wealth. For just a handful of change a day, a beautiful woman explained, you could significantly impact the lives of "little Tripti" and the "orphaned Rajesh," by sending them enough money to eat real meals and purchase schoolbooks. Who could argue with such a benevolent cause?

Clearly the problem wasn't the commercial itself, but the fact that all of my fellow third-graders had come away from it believing that India was only these things. India was disease, full stop. India was poverty. India was a land where no one could find either clean water to drink or clothes that weren't torn and dirty. It was indisputable: India was on the television set every afternoon, skinny and wailing and begging for help in between reruns of *The Love Boat* and *Gilligan's Island*.

Simply stated: nobody wants a public relations job at the age of eight. But that's exactly when I found myself launching my first spin campaign. Being Indian was a great point of pride, and having been to India three times by this point, it was my duty to change my friends' perceptions. After all, India was the most wondrous place I'd ever been and I was determined to let everyone know.

"India is thrilling!" I said. Then I told my friend Jeremy that my grandfather had once shot a wild tiger, and that the pelt was hanging high in his sitting room.

"India is rich!" I said to Zoe. Then I talked in great detail about a man who'd actually come to people's homes every Monday to iron all their clothes. I even told her about the servants, and the lovely aayah that would ply her with delicious flans and custards whenever she asked.

"India is exotic!" I cried out, to anyone who'd listen. I weaved tales of how you didn't have to go to the market by car in the villages. And while you could obviously take a car, why would you when there were Lambrettas, and autorickshaws and tongas, and all sorts of crazy vehicles I'd never seen in the States?

A week later, everyone wanted to move to India. But the fact is, I was selective in what I publicized, and there were things I kept mum about as well. I hadn't lied, but I hadn't been completely honest. And I still hadn't come to terms with certain things. Like why you needed to boil your water before you drank it from a tap. Or why you could play with the servants' children all day and walk around the streets with your arms linked, but once you came inside the same house, one of you would sit on the cold tile floor, the other on a couch.

The truth is, I spent years trying to make sense of these differences. I knew that India was a developing nation and was rife with poverty, disease, and corruption. I knew there were lingering class distinctions and caste barriers. And yet, I just wanted people to give equal weight to the positive. This was the land of Gandhi and Nehru and great mathematicians. It was a nation full of beautiful architecture, gorgeous landscapes, and mouthwatering foods. I quietly defended India in classroom discussions and schoolyard arguments, but I started to grow resentful. As I grew older, I hated that my friends were only moved by the worst in what they saw on their TV screens. I was dismissive of the myth that going East could help you find yourself. I hated the notion that some sort of two-week vacation through China, Tibet, and Nepal could somehow liberate you from your worries, and that life-altering realizations were just a visa application and a plane ticket away. After all, we had poor people in the States, didn't we? We had homeless in every major American city. Why couldn't people find themselves here? To me, it always seemed that this country wasn't free of corruption or drugs or class-ism. It's just that those things, well, they seemed to be hidden better. I made a point never to show my resentment. I never came across as strident or bitter, but I was. How could I know that, years later, I'd be encouraging people to make that same trip over to Asia because just such a trip — the most stereotypical in nature — had helped liberate me?

NOW

I am twenty-nine, teetering on thirty, and my life has been both peaks and valleys. At the age of twenty-seven, it was a series of valleys. As my friends were all graduating from law and med schools, getting married, having kids, and moving on, life was bullying me around. It was holding me down with one hand and punching me in the gut with the other. My girlfriend broke up with me. My favorite uncle passed away. My best friend from high school was dealing with severe drug problems. My debt was mounting. My eleven-month-old puppy got hit by the neighbor's car. Day after day, it only seemed to get worse. I'm not sure if you've ever had a period like this, but the three months after I turned twenty-seven left me a shell of a person, heart-broken. I felt one pick-up truck shy of being a country song.

But what got me through was my memories. In college, through a series of accidents, I ended up studying abroad in northern India, Nepal, and Tibet. I had no real desire to go initially, but after my friend planted the seed, I was intrigued by the idea of romping about the foothills of the Himalayas and looking for excitement.

My trip was filled with wonderful experiences. My study-abroad family couldn't have been sweeter. My mother knitted me thick wool socks and tried to fatten me up with delicious vegetarian meals, while my father ate meat on the sly. I drank with sherpas and had an interview with the Dalai Lama. I ate spicy potatoes with Tibetans as they invited me into their homes and taught me to sing their songs. I watched sky burials — sacred funeral ceremonies where vultures quietly devoured bodies from a mountaintop in minutes. I heard horrifying tales of surviving the Cultural Revolution. I crossed an ice-cold river naked while trying to track down a semi-nomadic tribe. I had adventures.

But the memory that truly persists is the one I wasn't looking for. When I was in India, something unforgettable happened to me. I was walking along a busy road with a friend, chatting, when I spotted something out of the corner of my eye. I saw a male leper, sitting on a stoop, asking a female leper to scratch his back. Neither of them had hands, and the woman hobbled over and started rubbing what was left of her limbs against the man's paper-thin shoulder blades. But what she was doing clearly wasn't helping, and though she was trying, he was desperate for the smallest satisfaction that a fingernail can provide. And on this busy road, people just kept walking, including myself. So, I kept on talking and then I suddenly realized my friend had disappeared. A second later I saw her scratching the leper's back. For a full minute I saw her make the tiniest gesture of humanity, touching someone no one else was willing to, and I witnessed the most beautiful smile on his face that I've ever seen. At that moment, my friend wasn't American, and she certainly wasn't Indian. She was just a human, scratching another human's back, selflessly.

Maybe it's just me, but I feel like my twenties weren't about making a difference in this world. I've spent the last decade selfishly: I've studied and traveled, chased professional dreams, and paid off debts. And it's bothered me that I haven't done more. I haven't volunteered enough. I haven't given enough money to charitable organizations. But what occurs to me now is that maybe I don't have to shoulder that guilt. Where time and money were scarce in my twenties, I'm hoping that my thirties will be different. Until then, however, I take comfort in the fact that it's these little gestures of humanity that can get us through.

As you turn thirty, I'd encourage you to look for the same thing. Travel. Escape your comfort zone. Forget the resort just once, and book a ticket to a place where you'll be confronted by differences in class and race and wealth. Because wherever you go, if you look just right, you'll see the same thing I did. Good people exist everywhere. And if you give yourself the chance to witness those moments, to really believe and dwell in and be inspired by them, you'll fuel a lifetime of happiness. Happy birthday.

2

Reach Outside Yourself

This groundbreaking philanthropist who co-founded Kiva finds inspiration in helping others — and shows how one can change the world with a great idea and the will to implement it.

by Jessica Jackley Flannery

Co-founder of microlending organization Kiva, Flannery believes microfinance, art of all kinds, and relationships are powerful tools for change. She is sector-agnostic about the origins of change, and prior to co-founding Kiva, worked in a variety of public, private, and nonprofit organizations. Jessica holds an MBA from Stanford Business School and a BA in Philosophy and Political Science from Bucknell University.

In high school, I went to Haiti for a week with my church youth group. The trip, during which we helped construct a building for an orphanage, completely blew my mind. After a few days there, I returned to my cozy suburban community, still in shock, and barely able to process what it meant to live in a world where some kids got cars on their sixteenth birthdays and others starved.

For a while, I'd suddenly start crying in the middle of malls and grocery stores, because I knew that many of the people I'd met in Haiti probably wouldn't even believe places like this existed. At senior prom a few weeks later, while watching everyone stepping out of limos and into the high school gymnasium in tuxes and fancy dresses, part of me felt like running around and yelling, "HOW CAN EVERYONE BE OKAY WITH THIS!? THE REST OF THE WORLD IS NOT LIKE THIS!"

I wanted to "do something" in response to what I now knew. I wanted it to be something big, something that would really change the reality I'd just experienced, but didn't know what or how.

Over the next few years, I went to college and studied the subjects I loved: philosophy and poetry and art. I also studied the subject I thought would help me answer my questions about why the world was the way it was, and then fix it: political science. Governments make all the rules, right? (It never crossed my mind to take a management course. I mean, I wanted to help people. Why in the world would I want to learn about business? What did that have to do with anything?) During my summers, I split my time between the practical and the beautiful, spending half my time in internships in the senator's office or at international relief and development nonprofits and the other half teaching art lessons.

Upon graduation, I moved to California and took a job at Stanford, in a research center called the Center for Social Innovation. I was really excited to be there, because I thought that being surrounded by great thinkers and new ideas about social entrepreneurship, philanthropy, environmental sustainability, and more would help me figure out where I might fit in the social or public sector. It did. In the fall of 2003, I heard Dr. Mohammad Yunus speak about microfinance, and I was hooked. This fit! It was a whole-body experience listening to his story. I knew in my gut I wanted to do the kind of things he had done, and he made it seem so possible. I could picture him walking around a village in Bangladesh, asking people about their lives, learning of their needs, reaching into his pocket and lending them the few dollars that would allow them to break free from the cycle of poverty that held them down. It was such a beautiful picture! Giving people access to small loans and other financial services, so that they could start or grow businesses and lift themselves out of poverty, made sense to me intellectually, emotionally, and spiritually. I wanted a chance to be a part of it.

A few months later, I got that chance. Brian Lehnen, the founder and executive director of Village Enterprise Fund, offered me the opportunity to work for him in Kenya, Uganda, and Tanzania for three months, interviewing entrepreneurs who had been given $100 by his organization to start a business. My task was to learn, and try to measure, how the grant had affected their lives and the lives of their families and communities. I would help them complete surveys, but was also given the "okay" to take photos and write mini-case studies/biographies about them. It was my dream job. I hopped on a plane as quickly as I could.

While I was in East Africa, not surprisingly, I became deeply moved by the stories of success each entrepreneur told me. Not every story was perfect, but they were the authentic stories of people's lives, and they were stories of hope and strength. Each one was triumphant, and fascinating, and poignant.

Simply being given a chance to succeed had changed these individuals in truly amazing ways. I saw that a relatively small amount of money could truly transform someone's life in a permanent and real way. And I had the privilege of seeing and experiencing what that meant up-close: a new home made of bricks or concrete instead of mud and thatch; a mosquito net; healthier food; parents who could now proudly afford to pay school fees for their children. Sometimes the details were smaller and didn't really fit on my impact-survey questionnaire very well. Elizabeth told me she was able to put sugar in her tea. Rose stood a little taller and made eye contact with people when she spoke. Joseph could finally afford a small padlock for the door of his home, in the middle of a slum, which made his family feel secure. I saw that even these things, which I couldn't measure, were meaningful and needed to be shared somehow, so I wrote them into my case studies.

Matt, my husband, came to visit me about a month into my work. He, too, became fascinated by the stories — actually, he had been fascinated by them for weeks, as I'd already told him many of them on the phone or over e-mail. Together, we began to think about how the world would be different if more people could hear these powerful, moving stories. It was an intoxicating idea, creating change by sharing something beautiful! We also began to realize that, if we could stay connected to some of the entrepreneurs we'd met, despite the distance separating us, we could continue to participate in their stories in an authentic way. There was an element of each person's story being a sort of cliffhanger — things had been going so well for so many of them, but what would happen next? We knew many of them could succeed if only they were given the next opportunity. Many of them needed a small loan next. Why couldn't we, and our friends and families, lend them some money? Why couldn't we leave a camera and a cell phone behind so they could tell us how things went along the way?

After a year of research, and talking with anyone who would give us the time of day about these ideas, we hadn't gathered a lot of support. Many experts said that what we wanted to do was illegal, others said it was just inefficient and not scalable, and others didn't accept that providing a small loan could possibly be more appropriate for someone than a gift or a donation. It was discouraging to get this feedback, but one thing remained true — our friends and family still supported and believed in us, as they had from the beginning. So, we decided just to start, and to start with them.

I returned to Uganda, and sought out one of our friends whom I'd met the previous year. He was a pastor in a small village near the Uganda-Kenya border, and a very forward-thinking guy. I gave him a camera, and asked him to take photos of a few of our other friends in his village who needed a loan, to write down their stories and their business loan needs, and to put these up online on a little Web site Matt had built, at www.kiva.org (kiva means unity). Matt's always been the one in our relationship who really can see the potential and power of technology to connect people, and he'd been able to build a simple, elegant, easy-to-use platform for this. Then, when I returned home, we spammed our wedding list with a request that they check out the site and consider lending. Forty-eight hours later, the $3,000 those businesses needed had come in, and we sent it along to Uganda. Over the next six months, we watched their businesses grow and were thrilled as they repaid their loans in full. Our experiment was a success.

After that first round of loans, we did a second, and a third, and eventually dozens more. We found more people to help. We signed up real organizations to work with us, administering the loans, collecting repayments, and updating lenders through the quickly expanding Web site. In our first official year of operation (which began the day our very first round of loans to Uganda ended, when the initial $3,000 was fully repaid), we did $500,000 in loans. In our second, it was just short of $17 million. Now Kiva does several million dollars in loans a month and has connected hundreds of thousands of people to one another in nearly a hundred countries. And every entrepreneur's story has a permanent home on the site, for everyone to see.

Something unexpected about this journey has been the sheer joy that I've felt at every stage along the way. The joy we felt when we started Kiva, and watched those first seven businesses succeed, was as complete and real as the joy we feel now, when Kiva is impacting so many more lives. It's true that scale is crucial to really address the big injustices in the world, but I also believe that just rallying your friends and trying your best to serve another group of friends together is meaningful and of ultimate significance in and of itself. And it's often the only way to begin.

Another thing I believe is that there is a very real power in unity. Regardless of political party or religion or culture, we can all be unified, and meaningfully connected to each other, if we focus on what is common among us. We hope that Kiva can create greater unity in the world, blurring the distinction between donor and recipient, and creating equal partnerships where both sides get to contribute to each other at different times. We hope to perpetuate the reality that there are intelligent, capable people everywhere. We hope Kiva can change the way the "rich" think about the "poor" — and vice versa.

I think it's very easy for some of us to build an insulated, isolated life where we avoid making the connections with other people that are uncomfortable, or messy, or make us feel vulnerable. But these are the connections that change us. Sometimes they turn out to be the most important interactions we may get to have on this earth.

It is my greatest hope that every one of us can take bold steps to change the world we live in, not by sitting back and thinking about how to "alleviate poverty" in some macro, zoomed-out, removed way, but by reaching out to a real, specific, individual human being . . . and then another, and another. In doing so, I hope we will each make a real exchange — not only of information and of resources, but of goodwill and common hope. Turning thirty is the perfect time to pursue this goal. It would be a true connection of our authentic selves. This is something every one of us can do. It will change us. It will change the world.

3

Turn Your Spirit Inside Out

The host of Trading Spaces notes that in your thirties it's time to pay attention to community: turn outward, look at the world around you, and see how you can truly make an impact.

by Paige Davis

Paige Davis is best known as the star of Trading Spaces, TV's groundbreaking design-reality show. Her book, Paige by Paige: A Year of Trading Spaces, made it to the top of the New York Times bestseller list. She has also starred on Broadway as Roxie Hart in the famed musical Chicago.

W hen I was asked to write an essay about "things to do when you turn thirty," my first thought was, "Why in the world would anyone care what I have to say about that?" My second thought was, "You goober-head! Haven't you learned anything about your own worth?!" I mean, really. Why suffer through your twenties if you can't come out the other side with a better grasp of who you are, what you think, and what you have to offer?

I spent my twenties searching for who I was: struggling to please my parents, my teachers, my peers. I thought I would discover who I should be by fitting into a predetermined mold — a mold no doubt fabricated in my own head, not one imposed on me by others. I was grasping for validation and affirmation from outside sources.

I don't know about fate or luck, but I do know about blessings. And I can tell you it was a true blessing that my tenure on *Trading Spaces* coincided with my thirties. Here I was on an unscripted reality show, so I was forced to rely only on myself. Literally. And guess what happened when I let go of all the pretending and was just "me" — my career exploded. I married the man of my dreams. My finances blossomed. Talk about validation! I no longer needed to reach outward for acceptance. I believe this is what allowed me to search inward for what I could give back.

My twenties had their place. But what I don't miss about those years was the nauseating focus on myself. My thirties have brought me a perspective of where I fit in the bigger picture of the world. There's a sweet irony to all of this. In one way I stopped looking outside myself, but at the same time I began to find what was important in the world outside of my singular existence.

I cannot walk down the street without thinking about my community and all those who live there. More than ever I feel the need to connect to those in my neighborhood — the butcher, the dry cleaner, the grocer. I even have a keener awareness of the homeless on the street. I feel the need to contribute, to let go of my narrow vision and connect in a grander way to those around me. My thirties have been the time to get over myself, and direct my focus on others.

One day on the subway I was struck with such sadness when I saw a homeless mother and her child pick up someone else's tossed McDonald's bag and tuck it into their own satchel. They were saving it for later. In that split second I knew I could no longer just talk about the homeless and fret over hunger in this country. I had to DO something, even if it was something simple. I researched soup kitchens, and found one only one block from my apartment. I volunteered immediately.

Working there on Saturday mornings keeps me in tune with my community.

I also devote time to other organizations and charities that help the homeless and the hungry. One of my favorite programs is Operation Backpack, sponsored by Volunteers of America. My neighbor works for VOA, and she is the one who got me involved. It is a program that delivers backpacks filled with school supplies to homeless children who desperately need a fresh start to the school year and who otherwise could feel embarrassed or, even worse, shamed on their first day. When she told me about the epidemic of 11,000 homeless school-aged children in New York City I could no longer just worry about my meager problems.

I think it is that redirected focus that has made me consider having a baby. Oh yes, you read correctly. Anyone who knows me knows that is a shocking statement to come from me. I've never wanted a baby. In fact, I declared to my parents and friends it was the last thing on my mind. But recently that has changed.

Even in my early thirties, my focus was solely on career, money, success, and my husband, Patrick. As much as people spoke about the experience of becoming a parent as being very positive, they also stressed that it changed everything. Well, Patrick and I have been very happy. We haven't wanted anything to change. Keeping everything just as it is has been fine with us.

But as I've stumbled along in my career, sometimes facing disappointments, the one thing that has upset me more than any stumbling block is the amount of time and energy I've wasted sulking about those things. I have become painfully aware that thoughts of career and success are not what I want to be occupying my mind. And I definitely don't want toxins of worry pumping through my body when there isn't even anything important to worry about. Heck, my career isn't even the most important thing in my life, let alone in the world. I very much want to pass on the love Patrick and I share to a little boy or girl, so they can have the chance to follow their dreams and discover their own passions and self. I feel that having a baby is kind of another way to "give back." Does that sound weird? Maybe it's not the most eloquent way to put it, but I hope you know what I mean.

It seems like I've written a lot of contradictions in this

essay. Look inward, look outward, focus on your own gifts, focus on others. Geez, maybe I don't have any of this figured out at all. But perhaps it's because all those things are linked. Lessons come in waves, and as people cycle through life they discover different things. But deep down I believe the key to happiness rests in learning your own worth, but then not hoarding the lessons for yourself. So get out there and volunteer. First volunteer to be all you can be, and then volunteer to give of yourself to others. And here's a dirty little secret . . . if you do that you'll feel like you're the one getting all the riches after all. ;-)

4

Harness the Power of Real Estate

This real estate entrepreneur illuminates how property can contribute to one's personal financial stability and a community's well-being.

by Bo Menkiti

Bo Menkiti is the founder and CEO of The Menkiti Group, an organization focused on enhancing the fabric of life in Washington, D.C.'s urban neighborhoods through the strategic development, management, and sale of real estate. A cum laude graduate of Harvard University, Menkiti was awarded the National Association of Realtors' prestigious "30 under 30" award, the Houston and Morland Awards for Public Service and Social Action, as well as the City of Cambridge's Mack Davis Award for the highest service to the Cambridge community.

Thirty years may sound like a long time but they can go by pretty quickly. As you focus on what has happened over the past thirty years, at dreams deferred, it may also be a good time to think ahead to the next thirty. It's likely that some of your dreams for the future may involve financial independence for you and your loved ones, owning your own home, building a stronger and healthier community, and helping to cultivate a greener planet. Whatever you might want to accomplish over the next thirty years, it will probably be in your best interest to learn something about real estate.

You might ask, what does real estate have to do with my personal dreams for the future?

I believe that if real estate is understood and mastered, it can play a key role in facilitating dreams, whether it's taking full advantage of the benefits of homeownership; focusing on real estate Investment to build wealth over time; or unleashing the power of real estate to develop the community, create social change, and make the planet more healthy.

My real estate story officially began with the purchase of my first home when I was twenty-four years old. It was a large row house in what was then a rundown area of Washington, D.C. The home didn't have much going for it except that it had a lot of bedrooms . . . eight to be exact. And as a young person just out of college trying to manage the mortgage I made full use of that house's one true asset. I filled it with room-mates for a year, a month, or sometimes even a week. I was able to squeak by and managed to keep paying my mortgage every month.

Over the next few years I realized that by renting out the house, I was not only able to pay the mortgage, but generate a small income for myself as well. I quickly started to realize the potential of real estate as an investment vehicle.

Three years later when I took the leap out on my own to start my company I was able to fund the start-up costs with the equity that had been built up in that first house. With that small investment I was able to launch a company whose mission is to enhance the fabric of life in America's urban neighborhoods through the strategic development, management, and sale of middle-market residential and commercial property. Today, the company is working hard throughout the Washington, D.C. area to use homeownership and real estate as economic empowerment and development tools to improve life in underserved neighborhoods. That's my story. You might say, "Okay, but what does real estate have to do with my turning thirty?"

Owning one's home is usually the greatest source of asset creation for most American families. If you are still renting, it's worth considering the immediate tax benefits, future equity growth, and gradual appreciation of a home as a means of creating long-term financial stability and preparing for retirement.

Most people today purchase their home with a thirty-year mortgage. If turning thirty has caused you to look back over the past thirty years and wonder what the next thirty may have in store for you, it might be worth thinking about what it would be like to own your home free and clear by the time you turn sixty and begin retirement.

Given the fact that real estate is a long-term asset and most powerful when its impact is looked at over extended periods of time, thirty may be the perfect time to learn more about the ways in which real estate can impact your life.

For many people, real estate can serve as an excellent investment vehicle. Whether it's by turning your basement into a rental unit, or through ownership of a single rental property or diverse commercial real estate holdings there are four key elements that make real estate a valuable source of investment:

• **The benefit of cash flow** that is available to you once the operating expenses and debt service on the property have been paid.

• **The benefit of appreciation.** While the real estate market fluctuates from year to year and experiences cycles of growth and decline, one can safely assume a 3-4 percent appreciation level over time once appreciation is adjusted for inflation. The average single family home in the U.S. has increased by over 8 percent a year since 1970. And while location, condition, and general economic cycles play a role, the rules of supply and demand coupled with our increased immigration patterns and limited land supply make a modest level of appreciation a solid bet over a fifteen to thirty year timeframe.

• **The benefit of building up equity.** Over time, as you

pay your mortgage, a portion of your payment goes towards interest while the remaining portion goes towards paying off your outstanding debt, gradually increasing your equity in the property.

• **The benefit of tax savings.** The Tax Code allows you to depreciate your property over a period of time and to take deductions for mortgage interest paid which can provide property owners with significant tax deductions.

Real estate can also play a significant role as a potential career path. The real estate industry is changing rapidly and the current average age of realtors in the United States is over fifty-two years of age and has been increasing steadily since 1978. What this means is that during the next decade a number of realtors and brokers will be retiring, leaving plenty of opportunities for a new generation of real estate professionals to enter the field and shape the ever-changing future of the industry. In addition to the brokerage industry there are numerous other rapidly growing and changing fields that involve the design, development, and construction of real estate.

Another potential role for real estate — and one I am especially interested in — is its ability to shape the social and economic landscape of our communities. Since shelter is a basic need, it's important that safe and healthy living environments are created. Construction and development are major sectors of our company and they have the potential to play a role in terms of job creation and the economic vitality of our communities. Since buildings are one of the largest consumers of energy in our country, the way we utilize that energy can lead the way in conservation and the greening of our planet.

I think the preamble to the Realtor Code of Ethics puts it best:

"Under all is the land. Upon its wise utilization and widely allocated ownership depend the survival and growth of free institutions and of our civilization. . . . the interests of the nation and its citizens require the highest and best use of the land and the widest distribution of land ownership. They require the creation of adequate housing, the building of functioning cities, the development of productive industries and farms, and the preservation of a healthful environment."

I have learned a lot in my first thirty years about the ways in which real estate can impact one's life and the lives of others and serve as a tool for positive economic and social change in our country's underserved neighborhoods. We can influence the environment we live in on a local level (our neighborhood) as well as on a global level (dealing with climate change).

When I drive down the street in Washington, D.C. or travel to other cities and states across the country I pay attention to the omnipresent nature of real estate. It is a powerful thread that helps weave together the tapestry of our lives. My sincere hope is that as you set out on this next phase of your life's journey, you take a little bit of time and invest in learning more about real estate. Who knows? It may just be the vehicle for rediscovering some dreams deferred from the first thirty years of your life — or discovering dreams for your future.

Section

PURSUE YOUR PASSION AND PURPOSE

5

Question Assumptions

This bestselling author of *The 4-Hour Workweek* urges people to work less, enjoy themselves more, and reclaim their purpose by designing their ideal lifestyle — not by obeying conventional wisdom, but by striking out on their own.

by Timothy Ferriss

Nominated as one of *Fast Company's* "Most Innovative Business People of 2007," Timothy Ferriss is author of the #1 bestseller *The Four-Hour Workweek.* He has been featured in the *New York Times*, the *Economist*, *Time*, *Forbes*, *Fortune*, *Maxim*, *Wired*, and other media. Tim has been invited to speak at such companies and institutions as Google, MIT, Harvard Business School, PayPal, Ask.com, and Princeton University. He speaks six languages, runs a multinational firm from wireless locations worldwide, is the first American in history to hold a Guinness World Record in tango, and has been a national Chinese kickboxing champion, and an actor on a hit series in Mainland China and Hong Kong. He is thirty years old.

Ignore the criticisms and suggestions of small-minded people, even well-intentioned ones. You can never please everyone, so don't try, particularly those who seek to make you "realistic." The perfect time to start doing this, if you haven't already, is when you turn thirty.

I started questioning the self-limiting assumptions of others, all the 'shoulds' and 'have-tos,' at the age of fifteen as a competitive wrestler. I'd been born prematurely, and my left lung had collapsed. I'm only able to use one-third to one-half of that lung well, which limits me from an endurance standpoint.

I also overheat easily since I can't dissipate heat, which is a significant handicap in any sport.

To compensate, I focused on techniques and strategies that leveraged power as opposed to stamina. I also had to train in such a manner that I didn't suffer heat stroke, monitoring my body temperature and maintaining a specific body-weight-to-skin-surface-area ratio.

In the end, against the odds, I became a collegiate all-American wrestler in 1995. In 1999, I won the national Chinese kickboxing championships with four weeks of preparation. These successes — and dozens of others, including a Guinness World Record — were due to testing assumptions others accepted at face value, not natural abilities.

Whether it's in sports, in business, or in relationships, there is an abundance of obsolete dogma, the equivalent of old wives' tales that refuse to die. This dogma — "the rules" — is passed from one person to the next without ever being questioned to see if it withstands real-world field testing. It's critical to test all assumptions and test them often. Times change.

When people tell you that you can't do something, it's important to keep a basic question in mind: What's the worst thing that could happen? If you're risking a small or transient failure for a potentially life-altering permanent benefit, it's almost always in your best interest to experiment.

Take my first book, *The 4-Hour Workweek*, as a recent example, which has now been a #1 *New York Times* bestseller, #1 *Wall Street Journal* bestseller, and #1 *BusinessWeek* bestseller. It was turned down by thirteen out of fourteen publishers, and by the first four agents I spoke to. When it finally sold, I remember speaking with the president of one of the largest online booksellers in the U.S. (not Amazon.com or Barnes &

Noble). I proposed that we do a marketing partnership, and I explained the specific plans I had for hitting the bestseller lists and creating a national phenomenon.

His response was, in a nutshell: I needed to reset my expectations. He said, "Let me tell you how this business works," and he later e-mailed me a PDF with sales numbers for the *New York Times* and *Wall Street Journal* bestseller lists, which implied — based on the statistics — that it wouldn't and couldn't happen. That was the end of the conversation.

If I had listened to him, and reset my expectations — and therefore lowered my efforts — it would've become a self-fulfilling prophecy. I don't think the book would've succeeded. It's now been on the *Wall Street Journal* list for more than sixty weeks unbroken, has been sold into more than thirty languages, and became a *New York Times* bestseller in its first week with no offline PR or advertising.

There are always more critics in the world than supporters.

It's important to listen to people who've done what you're trying to do, and not to those who speculate.

If someone regrets not having taken advantage of opportunities themselves, then there are two things they can do to make themselves feel better:

The first option is to put in the effort to accomplish what they've always wanted to accomplish. This is hard.

The second is to encourage others to lower their expectations and efforts, as this allows small thinkers to feel equal or even superior.

Most people are more fearful of disappointment than they are hungry for unusual achievement. Top performers in almost all fields have a common characteristic: they define risk differently than other people. Few things are high-risk if "risk" is defined as the likelihood of an irreversible negative outcome. If you frame things in the right perspective, you'll be incentivized to make mistakes of ambition, and not mistakes of sloth.

John Buxton, my high school wrestling coach, is one mentor who helped me shape these philosophies. He led by example and illustrated the importance of focusing on a limited number of adaptable principles, rather than on a thousand different techniques, as the best way to dominate any skill. In four years of competitive wrestling at Brown University, he wasn't pinned a single time.

Professor Ed Zschau, my professor of high-tech entrepreneurship at Princeton, is another example of an assumption-tester who leads by example. He's been a congressman, the head of IBM data storage, a professor at Harvard Business School, and a competitive figure skater, among other things. His motto is "Do it your own way," and he's insistent on teaching his students to test so-called common knowledge, which is usually incorrect or self-limiting.

One current example: I'd like to completely redesign public-school education in the U.S., especially in the areas of math and science. I'd like to double the number of science majors in America in the next ten years. Most (but not all) people in the education field tell me that this is impossible. They may very well be right. But that assumption has never really been tested. To me, it's a matter of thinking globally and acting locally; not in order to beat the Chinese or the Indians, but in order to contribute trained critical thinkers to the world.

You will not always succeed in your ventures. In the

business world, the first product I created sold close to zero copies, and I lost all of my initial investment. That said, I always test small, so if I fail, it's a fast and affordable failure. Micro-test, fail forward, and follow what works, not what you "know" (i.e., guess) will work. As Thomas Watson, the founder of IBM once said about his formula for success: "It's quite simple, really. Double your rate of failure. You're thinking of failure as the enemy of success. But it isn't at all." Just limit the downside of small experiments, and the upside will take care of itself.

If you're designing your work style to react to everyone else in the world, you'll never get anything accomplished. Productivity is personal and there's no single method for success, but there is one sure method for failure and unhappiness: trying to please everyone and respond to them immediately. It is impossible. Train yourself to recognize others' manufactured emergencies and to keep your focus on the one project or success that could change everything. Co-worker X likes to come into your cubicle unannounced to chat and is offended when you apologize and tell him you're on deadline or in the middle of something? So what? Pleasing him is the path to becoming him.

Let small, bad things happen so that you can accomplish the huge, positive things.

Finally, remember that you'll run into the same type of naysayers and obstacle-creators every time you try anything ambitious in a new field.

I'm running into the same things in the education field that I did in publishing. No one ever gives you a 'get-out-of-jail-free' card. You will constantly have to prove yourself and prove doubters wrong.

But then again, that's all part of the fun.

6

Live for Today

This legendary Penn State football player recalls how a single moment on the field changed his life forever.

by Adam Taliaferro

Adam Taliaferro is a former football player whose unlikely recovery from a paralyzing spinal cord injury, sustained while playing cornerback for the Penn State Nittany Lions, gained national media attention. A book, *Miracle in the Making*, chronicles Taliaferro's paralysis and recovery. Now a law-school graduate, he has created his own foundation to help support others with spinal cord injuries. The Adam Taliaferro Foundation, created in 2001, raises over $80,000 a year.

I n life, people are always looking to *the future*. My advice for people turning thirty is: *live for today*. Don't think about years down the line, don't think about what you'll do when you retire, because you truly never know what tomorrow will bring.

I learned that the hard way. I was playing football as a freshman at Penn State University in 2000. During only the fifth game of my college career, we were playing Ohio State, and there were a couple of minutes left on the clock. The game was almost over. I was playing cornerback, and I made a tackle on Ohio State's running back, Jerry Westbrooks. The top of my helmet hit his knee and pushed my neck down; that moment I broke a vertebrae in my neck and bruised my spinal cord.

It left me paralyzed. I remember waking up on the ground, and I had the kind of feeling you get when your foot goes to sleep — but this was how my *entire* body felt from the neck down. I was still on the field, and the thought that I was paralyzed never even entered my head. You always think something like that is going to happen to someone else.

Everything went blurry after that, and I woke up in the hospital. That's when doctors told me how bad the injury actually was. In fact, they gave me a 3 percent chance of ever walking again. I could blink, and I could talk, but that was about it. For the first week or so I constantly asked myself, 'Why me? Why did this have to happen to me?'

But after I got through the shock of the initial injury, the questions that followed were, 'How am I going to get better? How do I overcome this?' My parents were key forces in keeping me positive. They kept me focused on what I could do, rather than what I couldn't. My mom was there in the hospital room every morning when I woke up, and she'd stay until the afternoon, when she had to pick up my brother from school. At that point, my dad would come in and stay until I fell asleep. So I had one parent there at all times, being my driving force, pushing me to get better each and every day.

I had my initial surgery at Ohio State, and then they airlifted me to a hospital in Philadelphia. I began my rehab there, and was an inpatient for about four months. It was about a month and a half after my surgery that I finally felt something. I was up late, after midnight, and I was trying to move my toe, because I was always attempting to move something. The nurse came into my room and said that I was actually moving my toe. I didn't even realize it because I didn't know I was able to do it.

That's a moment you just can't put into words. The

nurse was ecstatic, and she called my parents. They rushed into the hospital at 1:00 a.m., and then we called my old coach at Penn State, Joe Paterno. We called everyone we knew.

Soon I was able to take my first step. The doctors still aren't absolutely sure how I was able to recover. My dad's a firm believer in prayer, and he prayed like no other. I think the prayers of so many people did have something to do with it. I don't think anyone could have gotten through that injury without some divine help.

My coach and my team were great, too. Sometimes, coaches think of you as just a number but that wasn't the case at Penn State. Everyone from the athletic director to the school president motivated me to get better. I remember the first time Coach Paterno came to see me, he said, "I want you to lead our team out of the stadium tunnel for the first game next year." And that was before anyone knew that I would be able to walk again. When I heard him say that, I knew I was going to give it my best shot.

The first game of the next season was against the Miami Hurricanes, with over 100,000 fans. And I led my team out of the tunnel. Not only did I walk, I actually ran for the first time since my injury. Since then, I haven't been able to run again, but at that moment I was able to, maybe because of all the adrenaline. All my family, and everyone who helped with my recovery, were at the game that day. It was an amazing experience.

I stood on the sidelines for the rest of that game, and in fact for the rest of my college career because I became one of Coach Paterno's assistants. For the next four years I was able to remain a part of the team.

Ever since my recovery, I've lived for today and done things I would never have done before. I always had a fear of flying, but now I travel all the time and am going to Italy to experience everything that country has to offer. I'm now graduating from law school at Rutgers, and have been accepted for a job at a law firm in Philadelphia. And I started the Adam Taliaferro Foundation, along with my high-school coach. Because when I had my injury, everything was paid for by Penn State and the NCAA. A lot of people aren't as fortunate as I am, so the foundation helps people with spinal-cord injuries, whether buying a wheelchair for someone or installing a ramp in their home. We raise about $80,000 a year, and each year the foundation grows a little stronger.

So live for today and enjoy everything life has to offer. Some things in life, like my injury, we can't control. But if you have your family and you have your friends, that's a lot. I could've easily gotten down about my paralysis, but I always had someone there beside me, friends or family, keeping me positive.

Though my initial injury was a negative experience, everything since then has been very positive. I actually got a lot out of it. What I tell people is that when I wake up every morning, and am simply able to walk, that's good enough for me.

7

Feed Your Passion

Passion and purpose are the perfect Ingredients for this co-founder of a granola company that seeks to deliver a humanitarian message as well as healthy food.

by Jason Osborn

Co-founder of Feed Granola Co., a company that produces healthy, organic granola mixes that have become popular across the country, Jason Osborn was named one of *Inc.* magazine's top "30 under 30" entrepreneurs to watch. FEED's successful brand has been featured on CNBC's *The Big Idea* with Donny Deutsch, *The Rachael Ray Show*, and in the *New York Daily News*.

As you look at turning thirty, keep in mind some essential strategies that worked for me:

- *Follow your passion, whatever it is that keeps you up at night.*

- *Accept a challenge and set goals in the face of adversity.*

- *Take a risk and step outside of your comfort zone.*

- *Visualize a way to achieve your goals.*

- *Struggle and sacrifice in order to overcome the risk you have taken.*

- *Believe so that you run on instinct and determination.*

- *After you succeed, savor the satisfaction of knowing you've put forth your best efforts, and risked everything in the process.*

I believe life should be a collection of all these experiences, both good and bad. In my case, I became an entrepreneur before the age of thirty, but my path was full of unexpected twists and turns.

Upon college graduation, I secured a traditional job with an advertising agency in New York City. But after the devastation of September 11, 2001, I soon found myself without work, looking for a new position. While interviewing, I realized that I wanted to look for something much different than I had previously done — I just didn't know what! I knew the things I liked to do, but couldn't quite pinpoint what I loved to do, or what I was really passionate about.

I started working as a model and bartender to make ends

meet but knew that neither job was my life's passion. Although I traveled the world and met hundreds of interesting people, there was still something missing. It took me many long hours of serving drinks, waiting tables, and daydreaming to visualize what I wanted to do. But once I could see it, once I could feel it, I knew.

I liked to cook and food was the centerpiece of my family life. I was fortunate to have grown up in a loving family, where I learned about tradition, commitment, hard work, honesty, and integrity. Ironically, I learned about these values while sitting around the kitchen table! As I was now living on my own, I had more free time to spend experimenting with new flavors I learned about while traveling abroad. When I found myself devoting more time to cooking than ever before, I began to wonder if maybe, someday, I might run a small café where I could spend much of my time in the kitchen. That idea seemed to be too much of a long shot to even dream about — I could barely pay rent!

I continued experimenting in my West Village, New York City apartment, creating new recipes, and coming up with new ways to prepare simple foods. I cooked dishes I liked to eat. Strangely enough, one food I liked to eat was cereal. Could I make my own? Could I make it more nutritious than the ones I was eating? Could I make it taste even better?

After making my first batch of two pounds of granola, I decided to package it in jars and give it away as holiday gifts. I was so proud. It was something I made that gave me enjoyment, excitement. It was weird . . . It was different . . . It was great! Little did I know, but I had found my passion. I found that spark, that energy! It wasn't the granola, it wasn't the cooking, it was everything the granola represented. It was the creativity and craftsmanship and enjoyment. I found something special: I found my job.

My roommate and now business partner Jason Wright and I began making granola in our apartment kitchen and started passing it out to our friends in our neighborhood. We created such a demand that we worked our day jobs and then made granola in a rented commercial kitchen until 2:00 in the morning. Our greatest challenge then was flagging down a New York City taxi that late at night with fifty-pound boxes full of granola!

We knew nothing about starting a business, we knew nothing about the food industry, and we had very little money saved up. But what we did know and agree on was that if we wanted it badly enough, we could do it. I knew this is what I wanted and needed to do.

The FEED Granola Co. was born the summer of 2004. We changed our lifestyles, sacrificed time with our family and friends, lost sleep at night. We were committed to the idea that if we worked harder than our competitors, we would succeed. "No" was not an answer, but "belief" was. We "believed" in everything about FEED. We lived it, breathed it, and we ate it six times a day! We became what the FEED Granola Co. represents: honest, simple, believers. We knew we could do it, we just had to figure out how.

We started selling to one store in our neighborhood, then two, then three, then ten. We began to figure it out. We made mistakes, we stumbled, but we began making believers out of others by getting right back up on our feet. We set goals, achieved them, and then set new ones. We made decisions without looking back. We kept moving forward, kept making progress, and continued to build momentum. It is because of this that the FEED brand was officially launched in October of 2006 and is now available nationwide, and growing every day. We have a long road ahead, filled with good times and bad I'm sure, but I look forward to each and every moment.

Being instrumental in FEED Granola Company's evolution before the age of thirty was a tremendous experience for me. I have grown significantly as a businessman, but more importantly as a son, a brother, and a friend. My priorities have greatly been affected, allowing me to make better choices. My confidence has flourished, allowing me to feel proud of my decisions. My instincts have sharpened, enabling me to make those decisions more wisely. There is something powerful about creating something special that so many others can enjoy. But there is something even more powerful in knowing what it took to get there. Find your passion. Challenge yourself. Take a risk. Find a way.

FEED is my passion. I will work for FEED.

8

Dream Deeply

This innovative violinist and composer reveals the importance of dreaming big and dreaming often — and not just when we're children.

by Daniel Bernard Roumain

Daniel Bernard Roumain (DBR) has carved a reputation as a passionately innovative composer, performer, violinist, and band leader. Known for fusing his classical music roots with a myriad of soundscapes, DBR frequently collaborates with some of today's top artists including Philip Glass, Bill T. Jones, DJ Spooky, and Ryuichi Sakamoto.

Margate: then

I started playing the violin when I was five years old, in a small town in South Florida named Margate, at Margate Elementary School, which was part of a music education program and orchestra known as The Margate Strings. Like most memories, the events sometimes seem more like simple dreams.

It was a magical time of good food, discovery, hot sun, bright days, adventure and a neverending sense of revelation, compassion, courage, and community. Playing the violin was a calling, and to be sure, sometimes the instrument chooses you. I feel the violin "called my name," and my life was forever changed. As a professional composer and performer, I now make a good living composing original music, touring the world playing the violin, and running my own production and publishing companies. In many real ways, playing the violin both changed my life and saved my life.

But now, there is a question and a problem: how do I remain relevant within the music industry and sustain the success I have?

Embracing the Inevitable, "Soft" Consequences of Hard Changes

A friend of mine remarked, "We are all senior citizens-in-the-making practicing for our final performances." We are all getting older, and with that, our bodies and minds will change. But what of our spirit and soul? For me, these changes in our perception all contribute collectively to our individual wisdom and knowledge.

We all know that changes in our lives will happen, and I refer to the minor and major transitions in our lives as "hard changes" — that is, changes that come unexpectedly, seemingly without warning or reason. But the results and consequences of those changes, and how we perceive them, is entirely up to us to define, and how we define them can either be good (or soft) or not. I say "soft consequences" because I think that any change, no matter how dramatic or life-changing, is best accepted as something good and necessary and fluid, rather than something unnecessarily fixed, heavy, and "hard."

My mother recently lost her job. She was sixty-five years old, and had worked since she was a child. A Haitian immigrant, her work, identity, and pride were all bound to one another. The morning came when her position at the hospital was eliminated, and she was unceremoniously asked to leave after thirty-one years of dedicated service. At first, she saw this as a hard, fixed change that had little benefit and value. But within weeks, she realized she now had time to sleep late, exercise regularly, read, pray, meditate, take classes, and spend more hours with her loving husband, grandchild, and extended friends and family.

My mother now sees that the benefits of this imposed, hard change has led to many more comforting, soft changes for her and all of those closest to her.

A Healthy Relationship with Both Fear and Fearlessness

I'm a composer because I was more afraid not to be. As I get older, that doesn't change, and I'm willing to do just about anything to make my living making music. I'm simply not willing to compromise how I spend the hours of my days and the years of my life. But with courage and audacity, there can and even should be a healthy relationship with fear, and I use fear as an important motivational tool towards achieving my goals. Fear, in this instance, can alternately be defined as risk-taking, investing, and taking chances, and to have a career or run a business really means a willingness to run risks, daily.

Before I started DBR Music Productions, I, like most artists, surrendered 20 percent of my fees (in commission) to a management company that had little regard for my future success. I decided to take a risk and leave them, retaining the full promise of my fees. I continued to remove 20 percent of my fees, and saved this amount until I had enough capital to hire and work with a business partner who could help me start a production company that could seek and secure future engagements for me and other artists. It was a terrifying decision, to leave the safety and security of an established management company. But a healthy relationship with my own fear gives me the courage and fearlessness, to embrace the hard decisions that oftentimes must be made in order to move a career, company, or dreams forward.

Having Goals and Making Plans

I have always had goals, but I didn't always make plans towards achieving them. Now, for every goal that I have, I am sure to make detailed, practical plans to support it. As I get older, my past experiences allow me to refine and adjust my plans, while not compromising my goals.

For years, I have wanted to "diversify" my career and work in film, television, and the theater. I knew I would not be able to tour as an old man, and really didn't want to depend on live performances as my only source of income. Using the career of the celebrated composer Philip Glass as a model, I was able to observe his shift from a music performance-based career, to a music publishing-based career, and adapt it for my own purposes. I first contacted the agents of up-and-coming playwrights, and asked if any of their writers wanted to work with a composer on creating incidental music for any of their works. I put up ads as a "composer-for-hire" on craigslist and other online sites for young filmmakers in New York City. I had my present management company contact film and television music agents about any new projects. And I continued to keep my MySpace and YouTube pages current and as up-to-date as possible.

As a result of all of this, I am composing music for the Obie Award-winning playwright Daniel Beaty's next new play, *Resurrection*; I'm creating the soundtrack for a new documentary *Off and Running*; and I'm composing music for several projects for the the cable channel ESPN. Collectively, these projects will provide me with an ongoing source of income that will allow for more time at home and more exposure worldwide.

The Ability to Dream, Decide, and Do

Your thirties will probably be a time of transitions. I think the most important part of getting older, more than embracing the changes to your body and mind, will be your willingness to dream, your self-discipline to decide what your dreams are and will be, and your ability to do something to make those dreams a reality.

When we are young, we are almost expected to play and dream and fantasize. It's encouraged as a natural part of our development. Teachers call these exercises "role play," but I think we should ask ourselves what role can private daydreaming play in our public, professional lives? Unfortunately, these encouragements end as we grow older, though they don't have to. Whereas our parents, friends, and family once encouraged us to dream and desire, as we age we have to become our own cheerleaders, and ideally, cheer ourselves (and others) on! You should know that dreaming is a skill, and when you stop dreaming, you lose the ability to do it. When you stop doing it, I think a part of you just dies and hardens and falls apart. To me, dreaming is an exercise, an important daily regimen for the overall health of our minds and souls.

Margate: now

Margate, Florida is never far from me or my sense of home. I keep a picture of the house I grew up in with me at all times. I'm buying my own house there, and will spend at least one week each month in it. Margate was the place I first started playing the violin, and my earliest memories start there. But what I realize now is that in order to stay relevant and move ahead, I need to constantly return to those places where I feel most safe, where I'm free to remember who I was, who I am, and who I dream of becoming.

Like taking a breath, I dream deeply each and every day.

9

Take Stock

In the world according to Curly Girl, life is not just about what's left on your to-do list, but what you've already accomplished as well.

by Leigh Standley

Leigh Standley is the creator of Curly Girl Design (www.curlygirldesign.com), featuring whimsical and witty collages. She attended the University of Kansas School of Design and holds a BFA in Visual Communications. Her work has been featured on a popular line of calendars, cards and magnets, and in national design publications and regional art shows. She is quite certain that given a cape and a nice tiara, she could save the world.

My thirtieth birthday was an inconceivable date to me not too long ago. I remember making a pact with my best guy-friend in high school that if for some *unfortunate* reason we were still single when we turned thirty, (gasp!) we would just resign to marry each other, thus saving one another from the horrors of inevitable spinsterhood.

MAKE YOUR LIST

TAKE STOCK

to do:

- read Newspaper daily
- take my coffee Black
- Speak French (Fluently)
- keep a PLANT Alive
- See Venice before it sinks
- Grand Canyon
- Sing Sing Sing
- be Organized
- read More
- Send holiday cards (on time)
- Take salsa lessons

have done:

- Live By the Sea
- GET A DOG
- learn To cook
- STAY TRUE TO YOURSELF
- EAT CAKE for Breakfast
- Be Powerful & Strong
- EARN MY keep
- Row a marathon
- FALL in Love
- Graduate college
- SING KARAOKE
- DO YOGA

30

VENEZIA

before she started on this journey

Our respective thirtieth birthdates seemed so distant that we were certain to be living on the moon by then anyway . . . with our lunar life-partners, of course.

But there I was — single, well, unwed, on my thirtieth birthday.

And where was my friend?

At home with his wife.

Super.

I thought of all the things I promised myself I would do before that day: have my first child, backpack through Europe, see the Grand Canyon, lose twenty pounds, move to Paris indefinitely, go to graduate school, learn Italian (or let's face it, REALLY speak French), keep a plant alive, drive cross-country, sing in a professional choir, go to church regularly, learn how to take my coffee black like my dad, take salsa lessons, read the newspaper every day, be totally organized, see Venice before it sinks. . . This list could go on I'm sure, but to be honest, it started to make me sort of sweat

Besides the perspiration, this list began to give me a slightly panicky awareness of time passing too quickly. Had there really been TWELVE whole years after my eighteenth birthday? It seems like it was just, excuse the cliché, yesterday.

Or at least last week.

But my rational mind kicked in to soothe the panic. Mostly.

I realized that for all the things I did not get done, there are about thirteen that I did.

I did graduate from college (barely, I think), I repaid my student loans (again, barely), moved to a strange city, lived by the ocean, and fell in love. I rollerskated to work, traveled some, learned to do yoga, learned to do yoga regularly, made wonderful friends, bought a car (or two), fell in love again, sang karaoke, shot whiskey, hiked mountains, rowed a marathon, learned to cook, got a dog, earned my keep, started from scratch, made a living out of something I love, stayed true to myself, learned to be powerful, strong and honest, and occasionally ate cake for breakfast.

This list could go on too, but I decided to quit while I was feeling pretty proud of myself. I look forward to the next thirty years if they are going be the adventure these have been, and I hope Venice hangs in there.

10

Find Your Passion in Life

For NBA All-Star Chris Webber, stardom in his twenties was all about living for the moment. Now, looking to his mother as the ultimate role model, he sees that life is about far more than that.

by Chris Webber

Chris Webber recently capped his career as a basketball star for the NBA's Golden State Warriors. He's a five-time NBA All-Star, an NBA rebounding champion, NBA rookie of the year, and a #1 overall draft pick. As a collegian, he was NCAA Men's Basketball first team All-American, leading the University of Michigan Wolverines.

L ike most of us, during my twenties I enjoyed a stage of self-exploration and an understanding of "who I am" more through action than self-reflection. A lot of my decisions dealt with the "now." Maybe it was that excitement of youth and feeling of invincibility, maybe it was about enjoying life in that moment. Either way, I didn't always look towards the future. My concentration was on the "now."

Turning thirty helped me look more introspectively at my life. Though I didn't persecute myself for the mistakes of my twenties, I reflected on why those choices were made and what I could do so I wouldn't commit them again. I have always had an introspective soul. Even as a youth and teenager, I would reflect upon my mistakes and actions and analyze how I could do better. Could I have studied harder? Should I have made that shot?

The only way not to repeat mistakes is to recognize them in the first place. But this time was different. This time when I reflected, it was more about who I was and who I wanted to be, rather than what I had done. And at the wise old age of thirty-five, I discovered something very important: one needs to find a passion!

It can be one's career — which I've experienced — but it really should be outside of work. The older we get, the more we realize and become in tune with our passion or calling. It doesn't have to be a "save the world" goal, or to climb Mt. Kilimanjaro, but something that may have been whispered into our souls since we were young. As we age, we hear and recognize these voices once again. It is part of that innocence, love, and true joy we experienced as kids. We need to follow that voice. That is where our real happiness lies.

Through my years of competing in basketball and business, I have always been drawn to children. When I look back at my youth, I realize it was because of the role model my mother provided as an educator, that I now have the same passion she did in helping students. As her oldest child, I was her assistant for vacation bible school, summer camps, day care, and babysitting. The connection with that passion has always been there.

Children, after all, are our most precious asset. For me, the most important thing about turning thirty was that I renewed my commitment to supporting our youth through schools. I developed more than just an interest, but a real passion for working with children in poverty-stricken areas and helping them develop through education and job training, and by gaining greater self-knowledge. This is my passion. What will yours be?

Own It

Sometimes a "quarterlife crisis" can lead to one's true calling, as this popular author and TV host of *The Works* discovered.

by Daniel H. Wilson

Daniel H. Wilson is a roboticist, author, and host of the TV series *The Works* on the History Channel. He earned a Ph.D. in Robotics from Carnegie Mellon University in Pittsburgh. Wilson is the author of *How to Survive a Robot Uprising, Where's My Jetpack?* and *How to Build a Robot Army*, and his Web site is www.danielhwilson.com.

I t's called a quarterlife crisis. This is the point in your late twenties when you ultimately decide to go out and gather up all the symbols of adulthood: dogs, condos, babies, whatever it takes. Note that the quarterlife crisis is the opposite of a midlife crisis, when every last vestige of responsibility is traded for a 1965 Chevy Camaro. For me, it began the precise moment that I saw posters thumbtacked into the walls of my rented apartment and it occurred to me that maybe I should buy frames. Although the crisis may last for years, when it is over you will have become an honest-to-god real-life adult.

The question is whether you'll be happy.

It's easy to make life-altering decisions when you're young. Too easy. Fresh out of high school, I decide to go to college. I don't see a future in my job serving frozen yogurt to hyperactive children and the animate mannequins who sell makeup at Saks Fifth Avenue. I apply to two schools: Princeton University and the school up the street. On the considerably more complicated Princeton application I naïvely list "Chewbacca" as my ideal roommate.

I go to the school up the street.

Once there, I choose to study computer science. This decision is made entirely because I enjoy playing video games.

Brilliant.

Memories like this are why I don't consider a human being to be sentient until around age twenty-one. Before then, people function on impulses from the lower brain stem, optimism, and beginner's luck.

Four years later and it's potentially time to enter the real world. During a summer internship at a cubicle farm I find myself in a fluorescent-lit room with a dozen adults undergoing a team-building exercise in which we are forced to choose our totem animals. I learn two things: I am an "owl" type worker and I must absolutely, completely, and under no circumstances enter the working world at this time.

That means going to graduate school, but to study what?

It's a big decision and I make it in classic nerd fashion by treating my life as if it were a role-playing game. Not "role-playing" as in kinky college-age fun, but as in rolling-a-ten-sided-dice-and-attacking-with-my-sword-of-chaos. Poring over the list of graduate degrees seems just like creating a new character. Genetics has already completed much of my character creation: I'm human, male, and skinny. Now it's just a matter of which skills to pick.

I choose robotics. It's just a cool-sounding skill. I

mean, say the word out loud: robots.

Again, brilliant.

As a result of this decision — which literally took five minutes — I spend the next six years or so learning everything there is to know about robots. That's because in real life, you have to cash the checks that you write in your youth.

On the plus side, I dodge the working world and prolong my childhood by hiding in an ivory tower.

This is a period of alternating depression and euphoria. This is having a paper rejected from a conference and reading the scathing critiques while shopping at Wal-Mart at four in the morning for instant macaroni and cheese. This is having a grant proposal accepted by the National Science Foundation and celebrating by sneaking fast-food into the closest strip joint. It's studying behind your friends' backs to get ahead. This is a ride down a long dark tunnel and at the other end, just a pinprick of light, really, is the glimmer of a life somewhere as an adult.

Because someday, school has to end. There comes a time when there will be no more carrying two freshly sharpened pencils to early-morning tests, sweating out homework at the last minute with all the smartest Indian kids you can find, or studying near the middle of the library because too far forward and it's noisy, too far back and there may be some random scholar committing lewd acts on himself.

For a role-playing character, the possession of a fresh-ly minted Ph.D. in robotics is exceedingly handy for a variety of exciting jobs; you need one to pilot an energy-sword-wielding Gundam warrior or to repair a 100-ton Atlas BattleMech. For me, this degree means one of two things: industry or academia.

And thus begins a lifelong period of brain atrophy that is called adulthood. My intuition is that during this long gray period of the-rest-of-your-life, making childish decisions based on the things you love — role-playing games, sci-fi novels, and neat sounding words like "mechanized infantry" — will fail. These choices will leave you washed up, beached on your mother's couch.

This conundrum — to work or to play — constitutes the central question of the quarterlife crisis. Staring ahead, it's suddenly not so easy to commit to living the rest of your life. What if you don't like your life? In the practical terms that nobody likes to admit to, the barebones question is really quite simple: how can I find a way to avoid actually working for a living?

My first job interview is at a big technology firm. I step into a room overlooking a thriving cubicle metropolis. I turn around and walk out before my interviewer can arrive and ask me about my totem animal.

The next interview is much, much worse. I'm standing in front of a whiteboard with a marker in my hand, a blank expression on my face. If I nail this interview — which is a non-option at this point — I will become the lead artificial intelligence designer for the most popular video game of all time: Halo 3. A life-sized sculpture of the lead character stares at me from across the room. I look into his mirrored battle visor and see my own terrified face and realize that not only have I completely forgotten the ins and outs of memory management in the C++ programming language, but that even in the guise of making a really fun video game, this is still, unarguably and irrefutably, going to be a job for an adult that will take, you know, lots and lots of work.

With six months left before I'm done with school, I've got no job and no prospects. I'm paralyzed on the cusp of my own future. And so I give up. I let go of the life trajectory. I step back from responsible dreams of wearing a lab coat and making discoveries in clouds of chalk dust. I blur my eyes until work and play are indistinguishable from each other. I start thinking like a kid again — the same kind of kid I don't consider to be sentient.

I've been acting like a childish professional for the last half-decade, so why can't I become a professional child?

It starts at a bar called the Squirrel Cage. On the back of a New York City parking ticket (the font grows bigger with each successive reminder) I scrawl the words "How to Survive a Robot Uprising." Then I doodle robots for a half hour and get drunk and fiddle with my cell phone so I don't look lonely to anybody.

But these words and this doodle become a one-page hook that attracts a literary agent. This spurs the creation of a full-on book proposal which is surprisingly easy to write because it is exactly the same as writing a grant proposal, only with significantly less research.

This document creates a bidding war between publishers which results in my becoming an author.

This is a job title for an adult, but I'm still playing with robots.

That part is solved during a lunch with the Director of the Robotics Institute. He asks if I wrote the book on "school time." This line of discussion quickly creates what engineers call a forcing function, i.e., an immutable behavior-shaping constraint.

I defend my thesis three days before embarking on a book tour.

And just like that, my quarterlife crisis is over.

The way I see it, truly childish decisions are the purest and most selfish and are almost always based on what really makes you happy. Responsibly following through on those knee-jerk decisions, maybe at great cost and for years, is what makes us into adults. Today, I write books that are small and shiny and usually end up in bathrooms — but they're chock-full of role-playing scenarios, sci-fi, and great words like "mechanized infantry."

The surprising thing is that I'm even allowed to do something silly that I love. But a funny thing happens to anyone who does anything long enough, no matter what it may be . . . you become an expert. Being an expert doesn't mean that you know everything, it just means that you know more than almost everybody else — and people respect that.

Just like your thirtieth birthday, becoming an expert sort of creeps up on you.

The quarterlife crisis culminates just as you ride the planet around the sun for that magic third decade and you enter the club of people-who-are-taken-seriously. You realize that, at least in some limited domain, you know more than nearly everybody else. If you are persistent, honest, and own the things that you love, then those things accompany you into adulthood; they are there to continue to make you happy and, with luck, they will transform into something that will feed the dog, pay the mortgage, and send babies to school — whatever it takes.

Section

GET IN TOUCH WITH WHO YOU REALLY ARE

12

Buck Up, Look Good, and Explore Your Options

While many young people fear growing older, this queen of the blogosphere says you should embrace your thirties as the decade you truly come into your own.

by Rachel Sklar

Rachel Sklar, media editor at HuffingtonPost.com, became a full-time freelance writer after spending almost four years as a corporate lawyer in New York and Stockholm. Her work has been published in the *New York Times*, *Glamour*, the *Financial Times*, and numerous publications in her homeland of Canada, where she published her first book, A *Stroke of Luck: Life, Crisis and Rebirth of a Stroke Survivor.*

The first thing to do when you turn thirty is get over it. Seriously. Yes, you had fun in your twenties. Yes, you looked great. You were also, if I may, probably an idiot. Seriously, how many boneheaded things did you do? Probably too many to count — mistakes in relationships, mortifying professional gaffes, racking up debt, getting tattoos and/or piercings, throwing yourself after that extremely hot person who broke your heart. Looking back on it now, they weren't even that hot. God, you were an idiot.

The good news is, you're much smarter now! Welcome to your thirties, the decade where you have money, taste, and have actually started to figure out who the hell you are. That said, you can still dress like a kid (jeans and hoodies and short skirts) — not to mention date one (the men will do this anyway, girls, so you may as well have fun). You can also date an adult — or, even better, be one.

That's actually the dirty little secret of your thirties: growing up isn't that bad, after all. Heck, it's actually sort of awesome! Instead of a job you have a *career*, one where instead of panicking that you're going to screw up, you realize that you actually know what you're talking about. You're better at dating — or at least better at getting out of bad relationships (sometimes by dessert!). The good relationships are so much better, and not only because you're better at sex (okay, I'm not gonna lie, that's a big part of it) — but also because you both have so much more to offer each other, thanks to that extra decade of cultivating knowledge, interest, and skills (let's hope one of those skills is cooking — or even better, giving massages).

Yes, true, there is more responsibility — the flip side of owning your own place is a mortgage, 'tis true, but then again, no more fishing the roommate's hairball out of the shower drain (or hearing through paper-thin walls). And yes, commitment-phobes, this is usually where marriage and family come in, but the good news is that when it happens it's because you're actually, you know, ready (no disrespect to you, twenty-one-year-old lovebirds with two kids, I'm sure you're very self-actualized). And while biological truths are hard to ignore (sorry, ladies, the ovaries do not lie), our options in that area are better now than they ever were. God may have given us a biological clock, but science has given us a snooze button — or at least an option to shop at a MENSA sperm bank

Look, I'm not going to lie to you and say that your thirties are going to be perfect — that would be like saying life is perfect, and it's not. It's just that your thirties are pretty damn close — you're smarter, cooler, and richer than you've ever been, and with so much less angst. It's the latter we're going to talk about now. Angst may have been cool as a teenager and par for the course as a struggling twentysomething finding your way, but in your thirties, it just means you're neurotic. So buck up and consider a few of these tips — an entire decade sprawls before you, you might as well look good. And feel good. And not sound like an idiot.

Right then, here we go:

Find a designer that flatters you. This is first on the list because it's important. If you're a woman, it will save you tons of time and front-of-mirror agony. If you're a man, it will help you attract a woman. By the time you reach thirty you should have figured out that not everything looks good on you, even if you really really want it to. But that's not your fault, because you're hot; it's the designer's fault for not making clothes that fit. (Stella McCartney, I blame you.) There are labels that reliably look good, and you will save yourself a lot of time and last-minute pre-event stress if you figure that out. I am proud to say that I still own — and wear — a

Laundry by Shelli Segal dress that I bought in 1997 at age twenty-four. A whopping eleven years (and maybe a size or two) later, it still fits; I wore it to the Emmys last fall. (Fine, the News Emmys. But still.) There are designers out there who love curves and designers who expect you to diet and/or gastric bypass your way into their clothes. The litmus test is being able to put it on, zip it up and then dance all night without thinking about it again.

Men: buy a tux. The corollary to the above for men is, buy the goddamned tux. You are not a gangly teen heading to the prom, you are a man and you should be ready to step out at a moment's notice, like James Bond only hopefully not packing heat. (Ladies: If he's packing heat, you might want to reconsider. Unless you've always wanted an excuse to ask about that gun in his pocket.) And yes, actually, we will notice if you try to pass off a suit as black tie. Also, re-evaluate after a few years. Styles change, and so will you.

Weekend corollary to this, both sexes: you need jeans that look great on you. Find 'em, then buy three pairs. (p.s. to my ex-boyfriend Sven: those 501s you wore as a fourteen-year-old do not count.)

Also, shoes: this is mostly for the boys. Yes, we look. Go with basic, classic, and non-squeaky.

Read the paper, watch the news. Okay, so you look good. Now what? Do yourself a favor and know what's going on in the world. This is not only for your own edification, though that's important. It's because social situations can be stressful, and anxiety results from (a) not knowing what people are talking about and (b) not having anything to talk about. Being up on the world solves both those problems. It's old-fashioned, but the paper in the morning and a newscast at night will keep you on the ball. (News junkies, supplement as required.)

If I sound like your mother, I'm sorry; it's just that I've lived the difference. I moved to New York as a junior lawyer, got a subscription to the *New York Times*, and stepped over it every day, late and frenzied on my way to work. I had no news-consumption habits and spent a lot of time trying to play catch-up (but come on, four-day-old newspapers are not going to keep you from your Saturday). Starting work in media forced me to smarten up, and talking to smart people became so much more fun. Now I'm a bit of a blowhard, frankly, but it's much more fun than being a mute.

Get your finances in order. You know what's attractive? Someone who doesn't always need you to "spot them twenty." Widen that definition to include someone who doesn't squirm when it comes time to split the check. This advice is so basic, it's almost lame for me to include it. That said, it is by far the advice that most people ignore. That and the squeaky shoes.

I know that check-splitting is a fact of life, because sometimes you can't afford to subsidize your buddy's surf, turf, and night of steady drinking. That is precisely why you have to rule your bank account lest it rule you, so when you inevitably do get stuck with the tab, there's a cushion. (Don't worry, your thirties are a long decade, and you will definitely not leave as poor as you came in.)

Learn about wine. Just a bit. Just enough to order in a restaurant, show up to a dinner party, and stock a wine rack. Have at least six wine glasses, that match. Learn how to mix a few basic drinks. These are life skills. They will make your life easier and make you seem sophisticated, especially if the people around you are drunk.

Read books. There is more to the world than you, your job, and your life. There is also more to the world than the twenty-four-hour news cycle, blogs, newsfeeds and IMs. Books will round you out as a person, and make sure you're never fumbling when someone asks, "What's the last book you read?" There are people who will ask you that before an entire dinner party, and they will not be impressed when you sputter something about the Internet, because those kinds of people always think the Internet is code for porn. On the plus side, when the porn is in book form, it usually counts as literature. So there's that.

Work out, but not too hard. Ignore this if you're a hard-core marathoner; we don't speak the same language, anyway. I'm speaking to the couch potatoes, or even those of you who, like me, have the best intentions but can never cram a workout into the schedule (you may, like me, be sheepishly paying for a gym membership that is woefully underused). You can get away with that in your twenties and even your early thirties but don't bet against the house on this one. The flip side is, my friends who became active in their thirties look ten times better than they did in their twenties. Just don't get your ass used to that couch, it will repay you by getting used to your fat jeans.

Oh yeah, the "not too hard" part — sorry, pal, but between your ankles, knees, and back, you'd better be careful. Don't bet against the house on that one, either.

Learn something new. If you're thirty, that means you have an entire decade until you're forty. Can you imagine if you took piano lessons from age ten to twenty how good you'd be? Or tennis? Or motorcross racing? Look at how good the people on *Dancing with the Stars* got — that can be you! (At your cousin's wedding.) The point is, if it's too late to become awesome at something by thirty, it's not too late by, well, whenever it is you finally get good at it.

Corollary: Figure out if you like your job. No one can do this one for you. Sit down and think about it, hard. Is this what you want to spend the next few decades building? Because if not, switch jobs. Sure, it's scary, but a lot less scary than looking back on your life and realizing you spent every day doing something you hated. No one is going to install you in the CEO office or anchorman's chair or a starring role just because you wish it, but there are paths to success for hard-working, talented people.

The number-one comment I heard from people after I quit my job to write full-time was "you're so lucky." I replied, well, you can do it too! The most common response? "I don't know what I want to do." So, figure out what you want to do. Take it from someone on her second career.

By the way, Jon Stewart started hosting *The Daily Show* when he was thirty-seven.

Volunteer. Karma. As you get older you'll need it more and more.

Leave the continent. I have no idea how much money you make (but if you can afford to buy a guidebook to how to be thirty, presumably you have some discretionary income. Oh, you're reading this on the floor at Barnes & Noble? Smart). Either way, it is imperative that you experience something of the world. Go to a place where they speak another language. Eat the food. Talk to the people. See the sights. Figure out the payphones. It's really easy to stay in your comfort zone. Don't.

Stop complaining. Depending on who you are and what you do, all this advice may seem very prosaic. You may already be rich, fit, talented, well-traveled, well-read, and completely self-actualized. Congratulations, I'm not talking to you — I'm talking to the rest of us, who still have dreams of being our very best selves even while trying to keep it all together from day to day. The advice I've given is really in answer to the most common complaints I hear from people — myself included — every day. All of them boil down to the same thing: "I wish." This is the decade where you get from "I wish" to "I am," and I promise you, it's gonna be amazing.

13

Focus on the Positives

This real estate scion and publishing force climbed the corporate ladder by a young age, but it was a family crisis that taught him what was most important.

by Jared Kushner

Jared Kushner is a principal of Kushner Companies, a diversified private real estate organization. At twenty-seven, he has been involved in over $4.5 billion of real estate transactions. Additionally, Kushner is the chairman and publisher of the Observer Media Group, which includes in its holdings the venerable *New York Observer* and Politicker.com. Kushner graduated from Harvard University with Honors in 2003 and obtained his JD and MBA degrees from New York University in May, 2007.

Faced with bad news, you have a choice. You can allow negative thoughts to weigh you down and discourage you from pursuing your dreams. Or, you can realize how lucky you are to be alive and healthy and doing what you're doing. Focusing on positives allows you to charge forward in life, no matter what.

I learned this lesson when my father was arrested. He was caught up in a crazy situation, he made a bad decision, and as a result I saw my whole world change very quickly. I was twenty-two at the time, in law school and working in the Manhattan District Attorney's office. Suddenly, I had to reassess everything and take on new responsibilities in life.

At first, it looked as though I might have to drop out of school to take care of my father's company. I had to assume responsibility for many facets of his far-flung business interests while at the same time providing support to my shell-shocked family.

At the end of the day, I didn't drop out of school. But I did get up at 5:00 a.m. every day so I could work before and often after going to school. It added a tremendous amount of responsibilities to my life. But I remember thinking to myself each morning: I can focus on the reasons not to get out of bed, or I can focus on the 100 good reasons that I have to get up and fight.

I also made an effort to remember that no matter what challenges I faced personally, everyone has his or her own challenges in life. I remember sitting on the New York City subway one day, coming back from my summer job at the Manhattan D.A.'s office, and staying on the train well past my stop, forgetting the need to get off. I just looked at the different faces on that train, thinking that every one of those people had their own problems. It comes down to the question of how big they let their problems loom. The problems that seem big today could be very small tomorrow.

That's why it's so critical to focus on the positives. And to truly appreciate everything you have.

Much of that positive worldview came from the upbringing I had. My father never really spoke to me as though I was a child. He'd take me to business meetings back when I was just four years old, and around the dinner table we didn't talk about school or sports, we'd talk about business. Whenever I got in trouble in school as a little kid, my parents would ask me why. I'd say, 'This teacher hates me," and they'd simply respond, "If the teacher hates you, then figure out a way to change that." What did I learn? That I had to focus on the things I can change, that just complaining about the world is a waste of energy.

The year before my father pleaded guilty in his case, I spent a lot of time with him in his offices, and talked to him twenty times a day. While he was in prison, I spent time with the company's top executives, learning how to make decisions and figuring out how to deal with people who were a lot older than I was. When you're at a multi-billion-dollar company and people have been running things a lot longer than you, you have to learn how to keep your thoughts to yourself when necessary. And if you do speak out, you'd better have thought seriously about the matter at hand, and feel confident that you've got something meaningful to add to the discussion. Because when you're the youngest person in the room, the first impression you make is very important. You have to be very respectful of people, listen to their viewpoints, and give everyone proper consideration. However, it is always important to trust your instincts and be mindful that new ideas and often controversial perspectives are the fuel of change and progress. These ideas will have more weight and a better chance of implementation once you have built the respect of your colleagues.

The same lessons hold true at the *New York Observer,* the newspaper I now publish. When I first learned the paper was for sale, I became so excited about what I could do with it that I saw all the problems as opportunities. Then, very quickly, those problems became my problems. But by being steadfast, focusing on what I could change, and not being worried about breaking some china once in a while, we were able to change the newspaper and make it run more efficiently. The *New York Observer* is one of the most literary and intellectually important newspapers and is read by the elite of New York and major industry. Before revamping the business, I worked hard with my team of professionals to revitalize the product and make it a newspaper of the twenty-first century. In fact, the *Observer* just had a monster quarter, with revenues up 61 percent over last year, an anomaly I am very proud of, especially since it occurred in a business that is generally in crisis.

While I have been fortunate to have gotten plenty of good advice from many well-intended people, the advice that touched me the most came from Rupert Murdoch when I was sitting with him right before he took over the Wall Street Journal. He was flipping through the Journal, showing me all the changes he was thinking of making. They were all great suggestions. But then he looked up at me and said nonchalantly, "We're going to make mistakes along the way. But hopefully, we'll be right more often than we're wrong. And if we are wrong, we'll be quick to correct our mistakes."

I thought to myself, this guy doesn't make mistakes. He's the best there is. But his words were a great affirmation for me. In almost everything I've done at the Observer and in other businesses, I've tried to follow my instincts. Sometimes my decisions may be wrong, but at least I'm making decisions. Being a good leader means making the right changes, keeping things moving along. And it means being open-minded enough so that when you're wrong, you can admit it. It also means never getting caught up in your own pride.

While I am very lucky to have seen a lot of exciting things in my twenty-seven years, I see every day as an opportunity to continue building a foundation for what I want to accomplish in the future. My advice to others is: learn from the best people, broaden your horizons, and never stop dreaming. In short, I have come to see that life is meant to be lived. If you find yourself unhappy with the status quo, don't just complain and be upset. Do something. So often my friends say to me, "My boss hates me" or "I don't like what I'm doing." Okay, then do something else. My parents taught me that lesson through tough love — it's up to you, and nobody else, to figure out how to fix what's wrong. When things aren't going the way you want them to, it is up to you alone, to figure out how to adapt.

Often, we tend to impose our own greatest limitations. We are the ones who limit what we think we're capable of doing. But sometimes, if you blow that top off and really dream, you can accomplish, build, and grow a life far beyond anything you had ever imagined.

14

Appreciate Each Step of the Journey

This popular motivational speaker and author — and former pro baseball player — learned how adversity can teach powerful lessons about life and appreciation.

by Mike Robbins

Mike Robbins is a popular motivational speaker, coach, and author of the bestselling *Focus on the Good Stuff*. As a former pro baseball player with the Kansas City Royals, Mike's sports career was flying high until he suffered an injury that abruptly ended his playing days. Through his own personal journey of self-discovery, he was able to move beyond the injury to find happiness and build stronger relationships. Mike and his work have been featured on ABC News, the Oprah and Friends radio network, in *Forbes* magazine and the *Washington Post*, and on more than 100 radio and TV stations in North America. His new book is *Be Yourself, Everyone Else Is Already Taken: The Power of Authenticity*.

I turned thirty on February 7, 2004. I remember feeling quite a mixture of emotions — excited about reaching this milestone in life, worried about what the future would hold and if I was on the right track, grateful for the love and support I had in my life, sad about some of the things I had not been able to do or accomplish that I thought I would by this time in my life, curious about what it would feel like to be in my thirties, and much more.

Turning thirty was, for me, a mixed bag. When I was a kid, people in their thirties seemed really old to me. Like most milestones in my life, getting there did not feel at all like I thought it would.

So much changed in my life during my twenties. When I was twenty-three my professional baseball career ended abruptly when I tore ligaments in my elbow and blew out my pitching arm. I was in my third season in the minor leagues with the Kansas City Royals. I'd played baseball since I was seven, was drafted out of high school by the New York Yankees, turned the Yankees down to play baseball at Stanford University, and then was drafted by the Royals. All I ever wanted to do since I was a little boy was to play in the Major Leagues.

After three surgeries on my arm and doing every-thing I could to come back and play, by the time I turned twenty-five it was obvious to me and my doctors that I would not be able to pitch professionally again. Although I was devastated, it turned out to be one of the greatest lessons of my life.

As I looked back on my eighteen years in competitive baseball I realized that I had only one major regret; I pushed myself so hard that I'd forgotten to enjoy the game. I was so focused on "making it" and on overcoming my weaknesses, I had not taken much time to appreciate myself or what I was doing along the way. We often waste way too much of our time and energy focusing on what we don't like, what we're worried about, or what we think needs to be fixed, changed, or enhanced about ourselves. We live in a culture obsessed with "bad stuff." Just turn on the news, listen to the conversations and negative attitudes of the people around you, or pay attention to the thoughts in your own head.

As we head into our thirties, most of us have become highly trained "human doings" (not human beings) who are obsessed with our results, hypercritical of ourselves, and working as hard as we can to "make it" in life, but forgetting to stop and appreciate what we're doing, the people around us, and who we are in the process. What if we stopped this negative obsession and started paying attention to what we appreciate about ourselves and life, right now? What if we took more time to enjoy and appreciate each step of our journey, instead of rushing around from one thing to the next — hoping it will all work out in the end? We will only ever be this age once and at some point we'll look back at this time in our lives as the "good old days."

Imagine how this simple but profound shift could transform your life, your family, your relationships, your career, your goals, and much more. Our experience is a function of what we focus on; each and every moment we have a choice about where we place our attention.

I am not advocating that you deny, avoid, or run from the challenges, issues, or the pain in your life and all around you. It's important that we're able to confront, face, and deal with these difficulties. However, we don't have to obsess about the "bad stuff" and let it run us. We each can consciously choose to focus on the good stuff in our lives, with others, and most importantly within ourselves.

Here are some principles for living your life in your

thirties with gratitude, authenticity, and ultimately fulfillment. They are the guidelines I do my best to live my own life by and ones I teach people in my speeches, seminars, books, and coaching sessions.

Five Principles for Living a Life of Fulfillment in Your Thirties

Be Grateful — Focus on the many blessings in your life and all that you have to be thankful for. This is often easier said than done, but gratitude is a foundational piece of living a fulfilling life at any age, especially in our thirties.

I had a conversation with a man from Ethiopia a few years ago. I asked him what he thought of people from our Western culture, given that he did not grow up here. He paused for a long time and then asked, "Can I be honest with you?" "Please," I said. "I think," the man said, "that people in this culture act like spoiled brats." "Really, what makes you say that?" I asked. He said, "Look, I'm from Ethiopia. Every day here is a good day." I was struck by the wisdom of his statement. Even though most of our lives are not perfect and some of us may even have some serious challenges we are facing, we all have lots of things to be grateful for, if we just take the time to pay attention to them.

Transform Your Fear — All of us have fear. The question is not whether or not we get scared; the question is how effective are we at dealing with our fear. Our physiological reaction to fear is exactly the same as it is to excitement. In other words, the chemical response within our bodies is identical whether we're scared or fired up. This is good news because it means that we can use the energy of our fear in a positive way, if we're able to transform it. The best way for us to do this is to simply admit that we're scared, even though we have been trained to pretend we aren't afraid most of the time. There is nothing wrong with being nervous, it is natural, normal, and healthy — unless you deny it (which most of us do, especially in our thirties, when we think we should know more or have more confidence than we actually do). Admitting your fear is the first step to transforming it. Second, take responsibility for what you're afraid of. In other words, own it — don't blame it on others or circumstances. Finally, focus on what you want and then go for it. As the title of the famous book by Susan Jeffers reminds us, "feel the fear and do it anyway." The only way to rise above your fear is to lean into it and go through it — you can't go around it or pretend it away.

Use Positive Words — Pay attention to the words you use with others, about things, and especially in speaking about yourself. Speak with the most positive words possible. Our words have the power to create, not just describe. We say all kinds of weird, negative stuff about life, others, and ourselves. Often we are not all that conscious about the words we use, but they have real power and they impact our moods, our relationships, and even our ability to make our goals and dreams happen. It's important that you say what you mean and mean what you say. At the same time remember we always have a choice about what we say and how we say it. Being happy, successful, and fulfilled is a choice and one of the ways we are able to create the kind of life we want is by using positive words in our interactions with others. Sometimes when my wife Michelle catches me speaking negatively about myself, she'll look at me and say, "Hey, don't talk about my husband like that. If someone else were talking about you that way I would get upset. Just because you are you, that doesn't give you the right to speak about yourself like that." What a great reminder!

Be Yourself — Oscar Wilde, the famous nineteenth-century writer said, "Be yourself, everyone else is already taken." Wow, what a powerful quote and message to all of us, especially while we're in our thirties. As we move through life, it's important to learn from others, get mentorship, and model the behavior of the people around us whom we respect and admire. Getting helpful advice and counsel is a healthy and empowering thing for us to do. Imitating others, however, is a completely different animal altogether. It not only devalues who we are and reinforces our notion that we aren't good enough; it doesn't work. There is and only ever will be one of you. And while none of us is "perfect," we're each unique and wonderful just as we are. Our culture these days is obsessed with what people are doing, saying, wearing, and more. So much time and energy is wasted on the latest celebrity gossip, trying to stay up with the latest hip fashions, or simply just wanting to be "cool." We are also bombarded by the media and advertisers telling us all the time that we are flawed, ugly, and need what they are selling in order to improve who we are, how we look, or what we do. Don't believe this!

As we enter our thirties, we have an important choice to make. We can continue down the path that many of us have followed from childhood, through adolescence, and into adulthood where we let other people's opinions or what is deemed popular dictate how we feel, what we do, and what we think is important. Or we can stand up, speak our truth, and do what feels right to us, with confidence, humility, and appreciation, being who we are as authentically as possible. This takes courage, for sure. When we live our lives in a way that is true to ourselves, we have access to real freedom and power.

Appreciate Yourself — Celebrate who you are, what you do, and the many gifts and talents you have. Self-appreciation is not arrogance; it's an awareness of your own power and the key to self-confidence, success, and fulfillment. Anyone who has ever achieved anything great in life and, more importantly, has created a real sense of peace and fulfillment for themselves, has an ability to appreciate who they are. Most of us, especially those of us in our thirties, are striving for external success — money, career success, marriage/ family, big house, nice car, exciting vacations, status, etc. While all of these things can be wonderful, none of them by themselves will make us happy. What we really want, even with all of the things we go after, is a sense of appreciation for who we are. In other words, we want to feel good about ourselves. The irony is that we have the ability to feel good about who we are at any time and for any reason. It's a personal choice that's always up to us. When we take the time to appreciate ourselves, not only are we giving ourselves a great gift, we're focusing on what we *really* want to begin with. And, when we appreciate ourselves, creating external success becomes much easier and more fun.

We don't have to wait until everything is handled. We don't have to wait until we get it all perfect. And we don't have to wait until life works out exactly as we want it to. We can start appreciating life and ourselves exactly as we are, right now.

From one "thirtysomething" to another, I honor and acknowledge you as you embark on this next adventure and decade of your life. With every passing year, there are both challenges and benefits associated with being the age we are. None of us have a choice about our age, but we all have a choice about how we relate to ourselves at each stage of life. My wish for you (and for me) is that we all take the time to appreciate each step of the journey and have as much fun as we can in the process!

15

Be a Realistic Dreamer

With much introspection, careful study of the Torah, and a chance encounter with a friend, this rabbi discovers how to be wise and practical while still holding on to his dreams.

by Rabbi Boruch Leff

Rabbi Boruch Leff is the author of three books on Jewish philosophy and a popular lecturer. Many of his hundreds of articles for Jewish philosophical journals appear at www.aish.com and at www.torah.org. He lives in Baltimore, Maryland with his wife and children.

I first heard the following quote attributed to George Bernard Shaw when I was age twenty-one trying to change "the system": "If at age 20 you are not a Communist then you have no heart. If at age 30 you are not a Capitalist then you have no brains." The lecture group at the college I attended was too large and did not meet as often as I felt necessary. While in full stride, complete with petitions in my hand, an older student said, "I'll sign the petition but nothing's gonna come of it."

"What do you mean?" I replied, "It is so logical and easy to implement. I am certain the university president will have to agree!"

"Alright," he shot back, "Time will tell. But just remember what George Bernard Shaw said and realize that you can't change the world."

The bomb hit at that moment and its impact has never quite ceased. This quote has haunted me since then. What could it really mean? If you think communism is right, why wouldn't you stick with it?

I recently celebrated my thirtieth birthday, the big 3-0. I now see clearly the truth of Shaw's statement. I initially learned this idea through Torah study; the kabbalist Nachmanides explains that all the world's wisdom can be found in the Torah. Afterwards, I also learned this idea through life experience.

Many are familiar with the biblical story of Joseph. In a dramatic turnaround, Joseph is transformed from jailed prisoner to prime minister of Egypt in a matter of hours. The Torah goes out of its way to tell us that Joseph was thirty years old when he began to rule over Egypt (Genesis 41:46). Why is this significant for us to know? The famous twelfth-century commentator Rashbam explains that at age thirty, one is "worthy of leadership." Interestingly, the minimum age to run for the U.S. Senate is also thirty. But what is so significant about being thirtysomething and being ready to lead?

I found the answer in a most unlikely place — studying the laws of Rosh Hashana. The Code of Jewish Law (O.C. 581:1) instructs congregations to seek certain qualities when choosing a cantor to lead the services on the High Holidays. One of these qualities is that he should be at least thirty years old. Why? The Mishna Brura explains that it is because a thirty-year-old is humble and broken-hearted, and can thus sincerely "pray from the heart."

It would seem that the Torah understands age thirty as a "moment of truth" when certain realities of life firmly take hold, and it is only through the acquisition of these realities that one can be a leader — whether in public life or in prayer. What might these realities be?

When I was twenty, the world was an open book. I felt as

if I could do anything and accomplish everything, while living on nothing. I would become a world-renowned personality — educating and inspiring, leading and loving — all without struggle.

Now that I have lived through my twenties and had many eye-opening experiences — jobs that brought lots of surprises, relationships that were difficult to foster and maintain, and neighbors that were a source of friction — I have become less idealistic about the world than I once was.

In many ways, my hopes and dreams of my twenties never materialized, and it is difficult to see when and if they ever will. I notice there are not so many people in the world that have the dream job, and most people do not feel as if they are maximizing their potential.

In short, things don't usually work out in life the way you thought and hoped they would.

As I reflect on this, I am indeed somewhat heart-broken and humbled. I was living now as a capitalist, a realist, as Shaw remarked. My 'communist' days, my idealistic days, had ended for the most part.

But then it dawned on me. Must I entirely abandon

my 'communism'? When one is first exposed to communistic ideas, they appear to be full of kindness and morals, expressing ideals to take care of all members of society without class envy. However, history has shown communism to be extremely impractical, leading to all sorts of evils and terrible abuses of power.

The lesson is clear. It may be true that you can't implement all your dreams; they may be impractical. But some of them could probably work.

As my birthday hit and I was pondering these thoughts, God sent a messenger to guide me. I bumped into a friend who said, "I just saw the greatest quote: 'If your memories exceed your dreams, the end is near.'"

So I have made a birthday resolution. I will still be a dreamer, but a more realistic dreamer. As a thirty-year-old, I am now "worthy of leadership." I can be wise and practical and not try to implement a hopeless fantasy scheme. I am humble and broken-hearted enough to know how to let go of senseless dreams.

Indeed, the Talmud (Pirkei Avot 5:26) declares: "At age thirty, one receives strength." This is the strength of character needed to pursue life's goals. The twenties' process of trial and error leads to a more secure decade of the thirties, when a person is focused on true talents, pursuable goals, and genuine accomplishments.

The old cliché is true: A jack-of-all-trades is a master of none. The twenties are the training ground to become a jack-of-all-trades. The thirties is the time to focus and master those talents that can be applied in practical directions.

Yes, George Bernard Shaw, how right you were. Post the big 3-0, I'm most definitely a realistic capitalist . . . but I'll always have a bit of 'communism' in me!

16

Go Hug Somebody

A senior Google executive, having lost a beloved partner, shares his touching thoughts about discovering what's truly important in life.

by Douglas Merrill

Douglas Merrill joined Google late in 2003 as senior director of information systems, leading multiple efforts including Google's 2004 IPO. Now vice president of engineering, he holds accountability for all internal engineering and support worldwide. Previously, Douglas was senior vice president at Charles Schwab and Co., and senior manager at Price Waterhouse.

D oesn't everyone have a big party of some sort when they turn thirty? I certainly did. I went out with friends to a bar in Long Beach. We had a lot of fun — great music, dancing, laughter, and way too much alcohol. I ended the night being sick out of the passenger window of a pickup truck to the cheers — and jeers — of my comrades.

It was a fitting end to my third decade. I had spent my twenties building a career, forming a life, learning how to be an adult. I learned a lot in college, but almost none of it had anything to do with being an adult. I spent much of the next decade demonstrating that I didn't know all that much about being a grown-up.

I think most of us are like that. We spend the decade between "teenager" and "never trust anyone over thirty" running as fast as we can toward something we can't quite touch but greatly desire. It's a great time to be alive.

Then, suddenly, we hit thirty. On my birthday, a friend said, "I feel much more comfortable in my thirties. I'm much better in my skin." I get that. My thirties feel much more adult, more human, and more … well … settled.

But it's not all about settling. The average first divorce takes place in your thirties. Many of us lose a job in our thirties — a real job that we cared about and wanted to succeed in. Life happens, for real.

This is also the decade when lots of us will have personal meltdowns or some kind of life crisis.

First, you try to manage these crises through action. You listen to sad songs and wonder how the songwriter knew your story. Some of us buy cars or motorcycles, and others find new "friends" (see first divorce, above). But I think most of these tactics don't really work. We will be overcome by "real life" events, won't be able to manage them by ourselves, and will need other people to help pull us through. For the first time since childhood, we need someone else.

In our twenties we are meant to be pretty independent. We're investing in ourselves, and growing as humans; we're not necessarily focused on core relationships with those around us. In fact, we may not know how to need, or be needed.

I certainly did not invest in the fundamentals of my relationships. At my core, I didn't know how to rely on someone else. And it turned out, I wasn't invincible either. I got a divorce and lost a job in my thirties. As for crisis management, I not only bought a fast car but also a motorcycle.

Of course, none of these taught me about needing people. Frankly, these events were all relatively manageable speed bumps. I tripped, fell, and rolled around like a beetle on its back. Before long, I figured out how to stand up again. Although really tough, these events didn't teach me any big lesson.

My big lesson in non-self-reliance happened at age thirty-five when my life partner, Jeanne, died. I learned I was nowhere near invincible, despite all illusions to the contrary.

My story with Jeanne, like almost all of my life's stories, begins at work. I had just transferred into a new department; I didn't know anyone, and barely knew anything about the new job. Jeanne was at my very first meeting. I saw a woman with a big smile on her face and huge blue eyes. She was so cute. She waved, and then ducked back behind the person she was sitting next to because she was shy.

We became friends, and ultimately more than that. Our first date was low-key. We went out for burgers at a San Francisco drive-in. She had a cheeseburger — ketchup and mustard only, please — and a milkshake. We laughed the entire time, about people, and places, and things. I was uncharacteristically shy. I didn't kiss her on the first date, although I found out later she had wanted me to.

Jeanne was always very interested in knowing me, not

just in being with me, so she usually had a question to ask, or a follow-up to something I said. Even when I was being childish, she tried to understand me. I learned a great deal about being kind, becoming interested in others, and being sensitive to their needs. Don't misunderstand; we were not the perfect couple. Though Jeanne was extremely empathetic, she was also as driven and goal-oriented as I was. Sometimes we clashed. As much as I loved her, ours was not a fairytale romance. We had tough times, too.

I was on a business trip during an especially rough patch in our relationship when my phone rang. A couple of days before I'd left, I had noticed a bit of yellow in Jeanne's eyes, and encouraged her to go see the doctor. She called to tell me she had seen her doctor — and had some answers. The yellow in her eyes was jaundice from bile backing up in her body. She had jaundice because she had cholangiocarcinoma.

My first reaction was "What is it? How do you spell that?" A quick Google search taught me that cholangiocarcinoma is a primary cancer of the bile duct.

It felt as if someone had punched me in the stomach,

and then did it again. And again.

But I swallowed hard and kept talking to her. Each fact we learned was scarier than the last. The prognosis for primary liver cancer isn't good. Generally, if they can't remove the tumor, chemotherapy is a common treatment.

As it turned out, Jeanne had an inoperable eight-centimeter mass in her bile duct. So we started making calls. Amazingly enough, a colleague's brother-in-law was an oncologist, and he referred us to one of the world's leading liver cancer specialists in our area. He ended up treating her.

Jeanne did go through chemotherapy. She went through so many surgeries I can't even remember them all. At the end, she had three different tubes in her. Because of one of the tubes, she couldn't lift more than five pounds with her right arm — and she was right-handed.

Her side effects were sometimes debilitating: A clot made its way from the tumor into the vein that flows through the liver. The clot caused back pressure in her venous system, which led to fluid building up in her legs. As a result, she was very swollen and in great pain. I'd constantly rub her feet and ankles. Even though it didn't make the swelling go down, it made her feel better.

Apparently, such clots are not uncommon in advanced liver cancer, and she had a quick surgery to put a stent in the vein to reduce the pressure. It was amazingly successful. In fact, two days later, all her swelling was gone. For a time, she was better.

She was so much better that we were able to go to a place she wanted to see again: the beach at Santa Monica. She was in a wheelchair to save her strength, but she was able to be there. I rolled her down the boardwalk to a spot between Venice and Santa Monica and sat on the bench and listened to her, and told her stories, and told her I loved her. I told her that a lot on that trip. We watched the sun go down over the pier, as the sun went down on our time together. I shall hold the memories of that moment, and her smiles, and the warmth of her hand in mine, forever.

A few weeks later, on the afternoon of June 23, Jeanne passed away. Her death was mostly very peaceful, but there were a few minutes where she was choking, and terrified. The nurse told me that I shouldn't do anything, just comfort her, and tell her it was all going to be okay. Of course, telling her didn't help — so I lifted her head. That did help. I was holding her hand, telling her I love her, and that it was time to let go, and that we'd all be okay. About ten minutes before she died, she opened her eyes, looked at me, and said, "Okay, it's time. I'm ready." I told her goodbye, that I loved her, and thanked her for being in my life. She smiled at me and said, "You told me you loved me enough." Then she died, still with that little smile on her face. She didn't die terrified.

That call from Jeanne when I was on a business trip was the start of this grown-up experience, but not the end. In fact, even her death wasn't the end, for me. Every day I miss her and think about her. I see actresses and random women on the street who remind me of her. I suspect this will be true for the rest of my life.

Among the thousand things I learned in my time with Jeanne, one key understanding was that alone, I was not enough to help her — we both needed help coping with her illness. We were blessed to have a really solid support group of family and friends. Her parents helped; several of her best friends did, too. Through our support group we found a great oncologist and a terrific home-care nurse. Jeanne had done a great job of building and sustaining her relationships with those around her. She was kind, gentle, and loving. She was honest and open, and focused on what mattered. She understood that her family and friends mattered. And so she had their help when she needed it.

In my twenties, I thought I was more or less invincible. I was building a career and an independent life. In my thirties, I've still been very lucky, but some of the speed bumps I hit were greater than I could handle alone. Jeanne's illness was a vast mountain, covered with snow and ice, inhabited by terrible monsters. She and I could not scale that mountain alone; we needed help. I can't imagine how much harder this experience would have been if Jeanne had not had such a strong support network.

Had I gotten sick instead of Jeanne, I might not have had such terrific support. Not because my family is not as "good," but because I know I haven't always invested in my friends and family. Instead, I tend to work too much.

Had I been sick, it's even possible that I would never have found the help I required. And even if I found the help, I would have had to work through a lot of issues before I could ask for help. That's a big "start-up cost" at a time when there's nothing to spare.

I haven't left my thirties yet, but I know how my friend felt: I'm more comfortable in my skin now. I certainly understand more than I did earlier. Thank you, Jeanne, for showing me the importance of family, friends, and relationships.

If I could change one thing when I turned thirty, I would go back and hug someone I cared about. I would apologize for slights I committed, ask for forgiveness, and forgive others for whatever had bothered me. I would invest a few less hours working, and a few more with my family and close friends. I would prepare myself to have the help I might need ahead of needing it. So put down the book, look around, and go hug somebody.

We'll be here when you get back.

17

Leave Behind Traditional Ways of Thinking

The editorial director of Billboard Group has her dream job, running the bible of the music industry — but her path wasn't always so clear . . . until she turned thirty.

by Tamara Conniff

Tamara Conniff oversees the Billboard Group's print and online editorial and design teams as well as *Billboard* magazine's industry events. Before joining Billboard in August 2004, she served as the music editor for the *Hollywood Reporter*. The daughter of Grammy-winning musician Ray Conniff, Tamara was born and raised in Hollywood, and has written for many publications, including the *Los Angeles Times* and the *Boston Globe*.

Twenty-nine was a bad year for me. A very bad year. My father was in the hospital dying. He was eighty-four years old. He had a good life, people told me. Sure he did, but he was still my dad, I was still only days from turning thirty. He wouldn't live to see me get married (if that ever happens); he wouldn't live to meet his grandchildren (if that ever happens). When I was sixteen years old, I had a plan. I was sure I'd have a career, be married, and at least have one child before twenty-eight. Best laid plans. Now I was twenty-nine, single, but had a career and soon-to-be dead dad. Thirty was looming over me like the end of the world. I thought I was some kind of female failure. Problem was, I didn't hear a biological clock. I didn't tick, like some of my other girlfriends. I had no baby time-bomb. But thirty — I was going to be an old spinster. Right? That's what people told me.

Then I turned thirty. I had no party. I didn't even talk to anyone. I actually went to the premiere of *Spider-Man*, figuring I'd at least do something memorable.

I woke up the next morning — thirty years old plus one day. And I felt deep relief. It was over. I was thirty. I wasn't twenty-nine. I wasn't "in my twenties." I was thirty and I was still alive. In fact, I wasn't only alive, I was an adult. Thirty carries weight. Somehow with a big "three" in front of your age, people can't mess with you anymore, 'cause you're not a child.

My father died five months later. Six months after that I moved back to New York City from Los Angeles to take over *Billboard*. My only regret is that he didn't live to see me have my dream job.

My twenties were about doubts. Who am I in the world? What should I be? During those years, I asked myself, 'What kind of life should I have?' not 'What kind of life do I want?' I made it to thirty without following the traditional path. So when I left my twenties behind me, I left traditional ways of thinking there, too.

Here's what I learned:

On business: I'm too busy to tell white lies to make people feel better. I'm too busy to suffer fools. I became very blunt and truthful. I spent too much of my twenties worrying about what people thought of me. Screw that.

On management: Treat everyone you work with or who works for you with respect. Yes, people work for a paycheck, but mostly they work for other people. Be kind. Also, never take anything in business personally. If you're wrong, admit you're wrong and move on.

On family: Spend time with your family. I spent time

with my dad when he was alive and healthy. It's time no one can take from me and thankfully, I live without regret because I did take the time to know him and love him.

On friendship: Most friends come and go — mainly because you or they choose different life paths. People go through a lot of changes in their twenties. It's okay to let people go. If you can count a few good friends on one hand — the ones you can call at 3:00 a.m., who will answer the phone and talk you off a ledge — you are a lucky person. Those are the friendships to nurture.

On love: If you've been in a string of bad relationships, its not because your partner was a bad person, it's because you chose poorly. Choose better. But don't be afraid. Love is a rollercoaster. Get on.

On marriage: You are not a failure if you are not married before you are thirty. You are not a failure if you decide to never get married. Choose the life you want, not what others want for you.

On children: Have a child because you want a child,

not because you want to fix your relationship or because you are lonely and it might be fun to have a kid. And, ladies, it's okay to not want children. It's okay to decide later in life you want one and adopt. You have options.

On health: Exercise, eat right, moisturize, wear sun block, sleep, don't drink too much. All I can say is at least I always moisturize and wear sun block.

On planning: Just say no. Don't do it. It's guaranteed — if you make a plan, something completely different will happen. The beauty of life is that you never actually know what is going to happen to you when you wake up in the morning. So don't get stuck in routines. Don't get stuck, period. Embrace change.

On money: Pay your bills on time. Invest. If you are not married, don't give your significant other access to your credit cards no matter how much you love him or her.

On choices: Every time you come to a crossroads ask yourself, 'Will I wake up in ten years and regret not taking this path?' That is the path to take.

On demons: We all have them. Talk to your demons. Get

to know them. Don't hang on to them. I never had demons that did not get the hell out of my life when I was strong enough to let it go.

On integrity: When you wake up in the morning, the only person you have to be able to look at in the mirror and accept is yourself. Choose accordingly.

On pain: Don't identify yourself by your pain or the bad things that have happened in your life. Bad things happen to everyone. In fact, there are millions of people who have been through worse than you. It's how you handle yourself that matters. Being a martyr is a bore.

I wouldn't take my twenties back for all the money in the world. I love being in my thirties. Enjoy.

18

Create a Screw-Up Fund

This acclaimed author and famed *New York Times* reporter reveals how she discovered an ingenious way to overcome her guilt for mistakes she made.

by Jennifer 8. Lee

Jennifer 8. Lee is a reporter for the *New York Times* and author of *The Fortune Cookie Chronicles*. She graduated from Harvard in 1999 with a degree in applied mathematics and economics, and studied at Beijing University. At the age of twenty-four, she was hired by the *New York Times*, where she is a metro reporter and has written a variety of stories on culture, poverty, and technology.

Right around the time I turned thirty, I came up with the idea of the "screw-up fund." It was a mental legerdemain, an Enron-style psychological accounting trick that made me a lot happier and eliminated a lot of stress in my life. I suggest you create one too, if you are the type to obsess over your mistakes.

The idea behind the screw-up fund was this: It was a line item in my spending — much like you might budget for rent, clothing, vacations, dining out — that basically absorbed the impact of my mistakes, of which there were many with financial consequences. If I lost my wallet (something that happened once a year or so), that was charged to the screw-up fund. If I got a parking ticket, that would just be charged to the screw-up fund. If I got a late fee because I forgot to do a bill payment on time, that would be charged to my catch-all account.

My screw-up fund was a way to let myself "buy" away my guilt for making a mistake, of just letting go and saying, 'Everyone messes up once in a while.' I mess up more than the average person, and now I have planned for it.

This was done in the same spirit that corporations do those massive "write-downs" on their quarterly earnings reports (which have gotten into the tens of billions, in the case of the mortgage-backed securities crisis of late). They write it down, admit their mistakes, and move on to the next quarter. Until, of course, there is another write-down, and the market frowns upon them again. But the idea is to make a mistake an event of the past.

Of course, my screw-up fund was never an actual set budget amount. Though if I had to guess, on average I probably charged anywhere between $400 to $1,000 a year to the fund, which (in my mind) was perfectly balanced by the fact that I didn't drink (I'm so sensitive to alcohol that cough syrup makes me tipsy). One friend, who loved bars and social cigarettes, did a back-of-the-envelope calculation that estimated that, compared to the average woman in New York City, I saved $2,000 a year between all the glasses of chardonnay and apple martinis that I never consumed. So my lack of drinking pays off in assuaging my carelessness-induced anxiety.

Before the screw-up fund, I would obsess and regret every time I made a mistake. Weeks for a parking ticket. Days for a lost wallet. Now I have mechanized the whole process of replacing a lost wallet, from ordering a new driver's license online to having a spare J. Crew magic wallet. And now I have a screw-up fund to mentally charge the lost cash and the replacement subway MetroCard.

My most expensive charge to the screw-up fund ever: Buying an entire new airplane ticket after I missed my plane to New York from Istanbul because I misread my itinerary. The next available flight for my cheap bulk class ticket on Delta was two days later, one day after I was supposed to be in Ann Arbor, Michigan to meet the Borders Books executives. I bought a ticket on British Airways at the airport, bit my tongue, and didn't look back. (Well, I looked back when I got my credit card statement, but not after that.)

The idea for the screw-up fund basically sprung up from my reading on happiness, particularly on the relationship between happiness and money, which became a trendy academic research subject and popular self-help topic shortly around the turn of the millennium. It is also branded "positive psychology" to make it sound more scientific.

Obsessing over something, having regrets, just continues to make you more upset. Moving on is good. Moving on from relationships ("It's called a break-up because it's broken"). Moving on from work errors. Moving on from social faux pas. This again, was similar to the corporate quarterly write-down. Move on.

The key piece of research that struck me (and inspired the screw-up fund): once you have enough income to maintain your dignity, there isn't really a correlation between money and happiness.

Basically, once people don't have to worry about where their next meal will come from, whether they will have a roof over their heads in the near and distant future, and whether they can dress decently, most have a homeostatic point of internal happiness. They return to it even if they win the lottery or are in a car accident. This lack of correlation between happiness and income is true not only within countries, but across countries as well. Adjusting for poverty rates, countries with higher gross domestic products (GDPs) are not necessarily happier than countries with lower GDPs.

What this basically meant for me was that having more money wasn't necessarily going to make me happier. But worrying about money was going to make me sadder. That realization, for a person who is relatively frugal, brought me to a greater level of self-awareness. It also helped me put the lives of my friends in context and to understand them better.

You notice that by the time you hit thirty, the life choices (and surprise jackpots) your friends make begin to manifest themselves in some stark ways: The tech entrepreneurs who sold their company to [insert Fortune 500 company here]; the Teach for America alums who started a charter school in [insert distressed urban neighborhood here]; the novelist whose first book is published nine years after she started it; the investment banker who now earns seven figures at a hedge fund; the doctor who moves to [insert African country here] to work with AIDS orphans; the lawyer who works at [insert high-powered but miserable law firm here]; the guy who hit it big on [insert reality television show here].

So you see the spread in terms of material things: the houses people buy (or can't afford to buy), the cars they drive, the vacations they take, the weddings they throw. At the same time you can see a range in terms of their satisfaction with work and their marriages (reflected in the number of divorces that occur).

Watching my friends, I learned that the people who were happiest were the ones who got to follow their passions, not the ones who made the most money.

One caveat: there are some who look at money as a way to "keep score." It is less about what money can buy than it is to see who is "winning in the game of life." These people are to be avoided.

What a lot of time-consuming, government-sponsored research has discovered is this: relationships and trust make us happy.

Insomuch as making money can help you build the quality and trust in your relationship, that is a good thing: taking memorable vacations together with your friends; having a shorter commute so you can have more time with your family; retiring earlier so you can spend time with your children.

When making money takes you away from your loved ones that is not a good thing. One consultant, who traveled often, decided to pull back on his career when his two-year-old son referred to the family's telephone as "Daddy."

Even as you head into the most important decade of setting your earning power/career path, I encourage you to be smart in allocating time with your friends, family, and loved ones. No one ever died thinking "I should have spent more time in the office."

Now I lay out my ultimate life equation:

Happiness = Reality − Expectations.

It's when expectations exceed reality that you get negative happiness, which is unhappiness.

So the key to happiness in life is managing expectations, which brings me back to my screw-up fund. It was all about managing expectations. If you expect to screw up here and there, you'll be less unhappy when you actually do.

Section

NURTURE YOUR BODY, MIND, AND SPIRIT

Kick the Caffeine Habit

As the chef and holistic health counselor who helped husband Morgan Spurlock detoxify and regain his health at the end of his *Super Size Me* experiment, this author knows from experience that fueling your body with the right stuff can lead to improvements in emotional, spiritual, and physical health.

by Alex Jamieson

Certified holistic health counselor Alex Jamieson offers personalized nutrition recommendations and support to her clients worldwide. She has appeared on *Oprah*, *30 Days*, *The National Health Test with Bryant Gumble*, and the hit documentary *Super Size Me*. Her book, *The Great American Detox Diet*, offers sane, tasty advice on how to cleanse, feel great, and live healthfully.

Those amazing years between living at home as a teenager and the true adult responsibilities of the thirties are often lived in a wild and caretree manner. My twenties could easily be referred to as my "health holiday." Working and playing hard, pushing my body to the limit, and feeling invincible — sound familiar? My twenty-year-old body knew no pain and I felt I could get away with some pretty bad habits. A cycle of caffeine all day and alcohol at social and work events at night seems very familiar to many thirty year olds — I know, because I lived it. Luckily, though I didn't realize it at the time, my body broke down and I had to find a way to heal myself and start a new way of living. Three, four, and five caffeinated drinks a day were starting to take a toll on my health in major ways. And I know I'm not alone. Take a good look at your coffee and tea habits — how about those slickly marketed "energy" drinks? Are you really giving yourself energy? Or are you robbing your body of the precious vitality that you need to be your most vibrant self?

We all know that caffeine offers us a mental boost, but what is it doing to the rest of the body? The overall consequences of regular coffee, soda, and tea consumption can be more harmful than most of us know. Until recently, modern medicine had not made the link between our morning cup and our deteriorating health. Evidence from recent studies has linked caffeine use with insulin resistance, adrenal exhaustion, liver and kidney problems, thyroid issues, and a sugar-craving cycle that seems unbreakable. Even casual consumption of caffeinated beverages has been shown to increase the risk of heart disease. Women especially should watch their caffeine habits, as caffeine causes valuable calcium to be lost through the urine. In addition, colas have a high phosphorus content, which also binds with calcium. Again, the calcium is leached out of the body through the urine, leading to increased risk of fractures and osteoporosis.

With all of this new knowledge in hand about what caffeine is and what it does to your body, you're probably thinking it would be a good idea to get off the "caffeine express" as soon as possible. And you would be right — except that detoxing from caffeine should be done with care. There is no doubt that a caffeine-free life is a better life for your health, but caffeine is a very tough habit to break. For most of us, the withdrawal symptoms that hit us as soon as we deprive ourselves of coffee make the idea of kicking it for good too daunting to contemplate. I remember my husband, Morgan Spurlock, going through a few days of serious withdrawal after he quit his McDonald's diet, and it was very hard to watch. If you choose to quit caffeine cold turkey, be forewarned: it may hurt. Literally. Caffeine constricts the blood vessels in the brain, and once you remove the caffeine, the veins flex open and the blood pours forth, causing a terrible (albeit harmless) headache. You may also experience body aches, stomach problems, irritability, depression, and fatigue. Be gentle with yourself — you have been using a powerful drug for a long time, and once you're no longer ingesting it, your body will react immediately and forcefully to its absence.

The best way to detox from caffeine is to do it slowly, by gradually decreasing your intake of the drug. Don't beat yourself up for not being able to quit in 1 day — if quitting caffeine were that easy, we would all be free of it!

Here are some proven techniques for getting caffeine out of your life. Remember, go easy on yourself, and set realistic goals for reducing your consumption over time. Start by going "half and half" with a half-decaf, half-regular cup of coffee. Drink your usual number of these half-mixes daily for the first four days. In addition, drink a cup of regular water, hot or cold, for every cup of coffee you drink. This will keep your body properly hydrated, as dehydration is a common source of fatigue. On day five, reduce the mixture to three-quarters decaf, one-quarter regular coffee. Continue this for another four days, continuing to drink a glass of water after each cup. Then you can make the switch to a full cup of decaf coffee, caffeine-free herbal, or other beverage. I recommend using "Swiss water process" decaffeinated coffee, which is processed with a nonchemical method of removing caffeine from the beans. Other decaffeination methods use chemicals in the process, and these chemicals are more likely to end up in your cup. The term "naturally decaffeinated" used on some brands of coffee is unregulated, so contact the manufacturer if you are unsure of whether or not they use chemicals in the decaffeination process.

For addicted tea drinkers, start weaning yourself by steeping your tea bag for less time. Alternate having a cup of regular tea with a cup of herbal or green tea, and you'll enjoy the same warm ritual without the caffeine. Continue working down your amount of black tea by replacing more and more cups with caffeine-free herbal tea or green tea. While green teas has one-third of the caffeine present in coffee, it also has a less bitter taste and has other beneficial effects on the body, so using it as a "transitional" drink while weaning yourself off of caffeine-rich black tea is a great option. Continue to hydrate with the following foods and liquids: good old-fashioned water, diluted fresh fruit and vegetable juices, herbal teas, soups, and whole fresh fruits and vegetables. Be aware that fruit juice has a high concentration of sugar, and sometimes people fall back on it as a crutch to get them through the caffeine blues.

Our culture has taught us to prefer and idolize beauty without effort, success without demands, and happiness without pain. In traditional Asian medical systems, light is always accompanied by the dark. It is the yin and yang of living. As winter proceeds into spring, our wholeness becomes defined by these contradictions of past and future, sour and sweet. Symptoms of withdrawal are a sign that the detoxification process is working — your body is releasing an artificial way of functioning and readjusting to its organic systems and state. If you think it would be helpful, allow yourself to retreat and care for yourself gently and kindly during this process. If you've been running yourself ragged on the treadmill of modern life, and you've used caffeine as the fuel to keep you going, it only makes sense that you may have to give yourself some space and time for detoxification to occur.

In addition to slowly reducing and eliminating caffeine, what can you do to perk yourself up, get yourself motivated, and feel energetic? Here are a few tips on how to get moving.

Hydrate, hydrate, hydrate. Drink plenty of water — get at least eight glasses a day.

Walk it off. Feeling droopy at work? Take ten minutes out of your lunch break to walk briskly around your building, to walk to your car and back, or to do a quick errand. Pumping your blood with oxygen, waking up your brain, and swinging your limbs will help awaken your body in a healthy way.

Lower and then eliminate your intake of refined sugar. By detoxifying your body of sugar and caffeine at the same time, you stand a better chance of getting into your body's natural rhythms and keeping your energy steady.

Stretch it out. Take two minutes at your desk to stretch your muscles. Raising your arms, touching your toes, arching your back, or twisting your trunk can give you a quick shot of energy to get you though the afternoon.

Deal with your stress. By facing and eliminating the areas of your life that are a source of stress, you will automatically feel lighter, more energetic, and less fatigued.

Look at your whole life and address those areas that are holding you back from being your amazing, ultimate self.

20

Get Fit, Get Real

Dynamic fitness instructor Amy Dixon knows what it takes to get in shape, and she knows all the excuses busy people have for putting fitness on hold. She writes about what thirty-year-olds can do to physically stay on top of their game.

by Amy Dixon

Amy Dixon is the fitness columnist and blogger for *Women's Health* magazine. She's an exercise physiologist and group fitness manager for Equinox in Santa Monica, California, and stars in several *Women's Health* workout DVDs. Dixon has been inspiring people to get fit for more than fifteen years.

Turning thirty unearthed an overwhelming drive for success and fitness in all avenues of my life. Soon after the birth of my second baby girl and during a time when I felt I was on the verge of "making it" in my career, my thirtieth birthday hit. After shedding the baby weight and recovering from a C-section, my daily focus quickly turned to trying to keep as many balls in the air as possible and then trying to determine which balls I was going to continue to juggle. I remember very clearly my mom, friends, colleagues, and acquaintances asking me the question: how are you going to do it? The "it" being: working a full-time job, teaching a full schedule of classes, training clients, being a mother of two growing daughters, managing a household, and last but certainly not least, being a supportive and loving wife of a man who in his own right has a challenging and demanding career. I answer their question every day just through my ability to get "it" done. I am noticing that as I explore and experience my thirties, my focus has gotten much clearer and fine-tuned on the things that matter to me. Family and friends aside, fitness makes up a huge part of my life. Fitness is so much a part of my life that I decided to dedicate my career to it, and it is the major reason that I am able to live a life of managed chaos.

The thirties are a time of transition in life and in the body. These critical years between twenty-nine and forty bring about the feeling that you'd better be on the right path in life, focusing on family and career, with the added stress of knowing that this is the decade to strap in, hang on, and hit the accelerator in both those areas. Physically, the thirties mark a time in the body where the metabolism starts to slow down, aerobic performance starts to diminish slightly, muscular strength plateaus and begins to decrease, flexibility decreases, and bone density for women can even start to decline.

The good news is that you can avoid the fitness and health traps of the thirties if you are willing to recognize how important physical activity really is and take this decade to truly maximize your level of fitness. And, most importantly, recognize that exercise alone has so many benefits. Physical activity can reduce the risk of chronic disease, help us sleep better, reduce stress and improve our mood, and lower body fat and increase lean muscle mass. With all of these amazing benefits associated with fitness, now is the time to set the precedent for your body and health with a mindset that fitness is just as important as all of the other balls you are juggling. Your health and quality of life are critical; your quest for success isn't worth anything if you can't enjoy it.

Here are my top five rules for approaching fitness in your thirties:

Don't fall for the all-or-nothing rule. More often than not, being able to balance life in a way that feels manageable often means excluding fitness and exercise due to a lack of time to squeeze it in. It doesn't make sense to do nothing just because you are unable to accomplish your goal (such as running for an hour) fully. This just isn't a good outlook when it comes to fitness. Remember that the intensity in which you exercise is just as important as the time. If you find yourself with thirty minutes to fit in a workout, go big and work at an uncomfortable level. Putting in thirty minutes at a level of intensity that is challenging and uncomfortable is every bit as good for your health as an easy breezy sixty minutes put in on the elliptical trainer or the recumbent bike. If it doesn't feel challenging, it isn't.

Make time. What I have noticed in my own household and among friends is that making the time for self in the midst of this decade can be very difficult. But what you must remember is that you have control of your time. You have the ability to say no to other commitments in order to make time for yourself. If you just hope that you will have enough time during the day to exercise but you don't actually schedule a time and commit, chances are you won't do it. I beg you not to get to a point in which you have to have your doctor tell you to exercise because your body and health are paying for your inactivity.

Variation in your routine is just as important as putting in the time. Once you have made the commitment to yourself to take time to exercise, make sure that you vary your workouts as often as possible. I would suggest changing up your program every month in order to avoid plateaus. This is when it is good to know what your baseline numbers are. I would strongly recommend meeting with a trainer in the beginning of your training to get an idea of where you are starting. Body fat and basic measurements are very important in seeing how far you have come. Ultimately, if your clothes are fitting more loosely, you are on the right track.

Drop the unrealistic expectations in the name of body image. Body image issues don't just apply to women anymore — I hear men talking about the same thing all the time. Images in the media and of celebrities affect all of us. If you want to make fitness a part of your life, get real with what you have been genetically blessed with and maximize your true potential.

Find out what works for you and then love it. There is no one-size-fits-all fitness program. Heaven knows that I don't love running long distances but I do love how the world looks from the seat of a bicycle. The fitness umbrella is pretty big. And the good news is that you might just surprise yourself and really fall in love with a new sport or activity.

I view fitness as an integral part of my life. Every single day I strive to be active. I work hard to educate and motivate my students and clients to achieve results, but I am also very realistic in my approach to fitness. It takes really hard work and dedication to feel good in your own skin. My entire belief system — not just in fitness but in life — is to get real. Above all else, getting real means being honest and true to yourself with what you want. Do what you love and have fun doing it. I am lucky enough to have a classroom of forty people depending on me to show up and give them a fun, challenging, and safe workout. But most importantly my time spent helping others get fit has helped me realize my own sense of innate fitness potential. I want others to know what it feels like to go breathless sprinting up a hill and to truly experience an exercise high, a feeling that is so far removed from stress and deadlines that you can see and live in the world more clearly. That is real to me.

Being in my thirties has allowed me to experience each day with a sense of focus that I have never had before. I'm working in a career that I love, I have two wonderful young daughters who show me what it is like to learn new things every day, and I get to tackle my thirties with a husband who drives me to be a better person. Since reaching the big 3-0, life has been absolutely amazing, and I plan on it getting better with time.

21

Seed Your Days with Exceptional Moments

One of the world's foremost innovators, Kumar suggests how to create quantum moments that can help you focus on the big picture.

by Dr. Vikram Sheel Kumar

Vikram Sheel Kumar is a pioneer in the field of community-based chronic disease management. In 1999, Vikram joined the MIT Media Laboratory and invented DiaBetNet, nominated as one of the top ten designs of the decade by *BusinessWorld* magazine. While in the M.D. program at the Harvard-MIT Division of Health Sciences and Technology, Vikram co-founded software consultancy Dimagi. In 2004, Vikram was named the MIT *Technology Review's* Humanitarian of the Year and one of the world's 100 top innovators.

It's very tempting in life to just fill your days with activities. Especially around this age, as you enter your thirties, it's tricky to avoid it: you're busy with family, you're busy with work, you have a lot of commitments picked up through your school and your profession. In fact you're gathering new commitments all the time, every day.

My main advice would be to not be busy just for the sake of being busy. It's pretty telling that a guy like Richard Feynman, the legendary American physicist, made his biggest discovery when he came back from a long trip. His colleagues had been working crazily on various projects related to quantum electrodynamics, but then he came back, had fresh insights, and was able to solve problems they'd been working on for a very long time. If you're busy for the sake of being busy, you don't have those opportunities to make such a quantum leap.

I realized this principle halfway through my undergraduate education. I had grown up in the U.S., but then moved to India at age ten, finished high school and some college there, and then moved back to the U.S. for medical school and residency. I saw that there was a group of students who would spend the whole week, and weekends too, working furiously. There was another group of us who realized that nothing really gets done until the last minute. So in a sense we could procrastinate consciously and accomplish as much as the others without wasting as much time.

With a lot of the things I've done in life, it seems like I'm racing at the very last minute, and I probably am. But I've also been thinking about the big picture, for weeks or months at a time. During that time it might seem to others that I'm not doing much, but I'm thinking about what I'm doing, and then I can execute quickly. It's the same with a lot of people in academia: They probably won't admit it, but they often give themselves only a couple of days to do something, and then they efficiently turn out something that is focused and complete.

Over the years, it's just become my style to focus very hard at the end of a project. I'm definitely clear on deadlines, and that forces me to be extremely focused. That way I'm able to take time for other things in life. I'm in India right now, and every day I'm playing for a couple of hours — cricket or squash or yoga. Later on, I'll be up late, maybe until 2:00 or 3:00 a.m., to get my work done. But by now I have a pretty good sense of how far I can push myself, and at least I won't have been sitting at a desk for five weeks in a row.

There's this great concept the Greeks had of kairos versus chronos time. Chronos is when you look at time in a linear pattern: It's finite, there are sixty seconds in a minute, there are only so many hours and days, and you can't change that. Kairos, the other concept, is about nonlinear time, rich moments and connections that are, in a way, beyond time. A lot of people get to their thirties or forties or fifties and are still fighting time, forgetting that each part of life has its beauty. I try to advise people to forget about chronos, which is impossible to change or defeat. Instead, work on developing kairos.

For instance, reading this essay might take you twenty minutes. But if someone out there has a couple of breakthrough moments as a result of something I've said, these words could last much longer. They'll be replayed in people's minds, and that way time is almost stretched. What I say to people is that they should seed their lives with moments of great connection, so they don't even need to care about chronos. You're not running that rat race anymore; it's happening on its own, and you can just sit back. You can't extend time, but what you can do is live a full life with moments so rich, and memories that are replayed forever, that they seem much longer than they actually were. It's kind of a planned randomness. Know how to appreciate true connections, and seed your days with exceptional moments, rather than worrying about the clock.

In my career, my quantum moments have come when I've been able to sit back and truly listen to other people. It's another way to look at business. I'm an entrepreneur, and it's very difficult to not want to do everything myself. But sometimes I see people who are so much better at the things I've been trying to do, and when I listen to and appreciate their vision, then we can take a quantum leap forward. One of the reasons I co-founded my software consulting company Dimagi was that I was working with someone exceptional, who was far smarter than any of the rest of us. He was interested in particular paths, and so we worked with him and built a company around him. When you look at the bigger picture, you can truly see where other people can fit in.

In the business world, don't take on projects just in order to keep busy. Give yourself some space to focus only on important and interesting problems, and wait until those arise. Our company's focus on rural health initiatives fit perfectly with that philosophy: other people were doing high-revenue projects that just weren't interesting to us. Then we came across the idea of rural health, and we didn't have to look any further, because hardly anyone else was even working in that field.

One of our quantum projects was that we designed a smartcard-based health system in Zambia that's now the country standard. Every patient in the country will get one of these cards. Projects like that begin with someone calling us with a big, bold idea, and then we have the resources and patience to make them become concrete. We can execute because we give ourselves the time to do small projects. We can look at opportunities that compel us, that we see as interesting and important even if there's not huge revenue in them. Then our biggest success will be when we can walk away from a finished project, and it can run on its own.

Sometimes our philosophy is frustrating for those who work for us, or with us. They may not get the sense of the bigger picture. So we're constantly selling our philosophy and way of thinking. Our motivation isn't purely money-driven. Most people think that being busy generates wealth, but it doesn't, and so we have to sell our own vision of life.

Our vision is that it's important in life to step back. Employees should close their doors once in a while, to think and write. You can't just transact all the time. You need to fill your life with moments where you're not transacting, but creating. That way you're not just moving meaningless bits around, and being busy for the sake of being busy. Instead you're creating, and designing, and building bigger plans. Then everything else falls into place.

22

Grab Hold of Opportunity and Go Outside Your Comfort Zone

Publishing wunderkind Vivek Shah has risen through the ranks at one company, while colleagues hopped from one job to the next. To him, loyalty is important but it doesn't mean becoming complacent.

by Vivek Shah

Vivek Shah is president of the Fortune|Money Group at Time Inc. Shah formerly served as president of digital publishing for the group, where he oversaw CNNMoney.com. Shah has been named Online Publisher of the Year by *min* magazine and Innovator of the Year by BtoB's (Business-to-Business) Media Business. Shah was also named to *Folio* magazine's "Thirty Under 30" list and *Crain's* "Forty Under 40" list.

I have a stack of "ding letters" from thirteen years ago in my attic. Ding letters, which have almost become extinct, are those perfunctory rejection letters from employers. The kind that "thank you for your interest" but declare, without even having met you in most instances, that your background "does not fit." My stack consists of correspondence from every single media company in the northeast corridor.

It was 1994 and I had just graduated from Tufts University in Massachusetts. I had been the editor-in-chief of two campus publications and started a third with some classmates, so it made all the sense in the world to me that I should get a job in media. The problem I came to quickly realize was that the media industry was emerging from some difficult years and that a twenty-one-year-old with zero professional experience — and no connections to speak of — wasn't going to easily land a job, let alone an interview.

The dings came in the mail one after another. So did my student loan statements. The trips to the mailbox took on a masochistic flavor. I was getting nervous, desperate even. I needed a lead. Some glimmer of hope. And then it came. I received a call from a recruiter at Time Inc., the biggest magazine publisher in the world. There was something in my "To Whom It May Concern" cover letter that motivated her to call. She asked me to come in.

We met and she saw something in me that she liked. She quickly set me up with someone who had a job opening at the company. He passed. She set up another interview. Pass, again. But she didn't give up and neither did I. Over the course of six months, I interviewed with eighteen people at Time Inc.! Either they didn't have an opening or I wasn't experienced enough or they just thought I didn't "fit." I hate that word. I even got a job offer from another magazine publisher but by then I was convinced that Time Inc. was the company for me even if that sentiment wasn't entirely mutual.

Then one spring day I received the call. *Fortune* magazine wanted to offer me a job. I accepted immediately and felt the delicious satisfaction that comes from perseverance and patience. I resolved to take full advantage of this opportunity and now that I was in the company of my dreams it was going to take a lot to get me out.

Today, thirteen years later, I'm still at Time Inc. as the president of *Fortune* and its sibling, *Money* magazine. We also operate the world's largest dedicated financial Web site, CNNMoney.com, in partnership with CNN. Our unit employs over five hundred people in eighteen cities throughout the world. It's a big, amazing job.

I'm a Gen X'er. My generation, and its successor generation, Gen Y, are known to be "fickle" and "hard to please." We're not known to be terribly loyal. We take a new job with a view to where it can take us next. The economy has been good. Really good in some years. There is always a better-paying job — be it down the hall or with a competitor. Along the way, we collect job titles and pay raises like stamps on a passport. Job-hopping has become the accepted and celebrated norm. And, in many instances, it's the right call.

But, I've worked at one company my entire professional career. If there's one thing I'd recommend you do before thirty: stick it out. Stay in one place long enough to see where it can take you. Patience and working at one company can become magically exponential. It's not enough, though, just to bide your time. You need to be proactive and create experiences and opportunities for yourself.

The first lesson I learned is that it's not always just about the job you're hired to do. When I started at *Fortune*, I had a job with specific responsibilities. I did every aspect of that job, but also started developing business ideas on the side. I worked late and on weekends to come up with ways to break through. After a couple of years, I had an idea that catapulted me into the limelight. It was a business that no one else had thought of at the company and it instantly generated profits for the magazine.

My goal has always been to add value by creating and doing things that would otherwise not be created or done. That is a clear path to business success, in my mind. It means going above and beyond, and creating value in unexpected and surprising ways. You can't wait for someone to ask you to do something. Grab hold of opportunity and act.

I was twenty-six when the head of my department at the time and his number two left the company. I was one of three managers who were suddenly left without supervisors. Each of us managed a team but none of us, it was thought, were ready to run the whole group. The then-president of Fortune pulled us together and said that he was going to quickly recruit a new department head from the outside, leaving unsaid what we managers all knew — each of us was too inexperienced to be legitimate candidates.

But I also knew that possession was nine-tenths of the law and that the president needed someone to step up during the transition to keep the wheels on the cart and the department moving in the right direction. So that's exactly what I did. To my surprise, most of my peers welcomed the leadership and having someone setting priorities and making sure things got done. The president got to see my management skills firsthand and within a few months decided to install me as the department head.

Not long after that came the siren song of the "dotcom" boom. Folks in the magazine industry started fleeing in droves to the "new, new thing" and many of them, it seemed, were joining outfits that were minting millionaires every day. Only later did we realize that the dotcom riches were more the exception than the rule, but at the time it felt like if you weren't taking the Internet plunge, then you were missing out on a sure thing.

I stayed put. Not because I wasn't getting multiple calls a day from headhunters (I was), but because I thought long and hard about that stack of ding letters. Did I want to trade everything I had worked for since then for what felt like a modern-day gold rush? Hadn't I seen the benefit of sticking it out?

Right when it felt like I had missed out on the greatest legal wealth creation of the twentieth century, the bubble burst. People were instantly out of jobs. The economy began to soften. I was grateful that I was in an incredibly satisfying and interesting job while a number of my former colleagues were out of work.

One day, the president of *Fortune* got promoted to a big corporate job and the magazine's general manager was promoted to president. My new boss invited me to dinner. I knew him well, as we had worked side by side for a number of years, and I figured he just wanted to talk strategy and get my thoughts about the magazine. Before our appetizers were served, he offered me his old job, to be general manager of the magazine.

I didn't quite know how to react. On the one hand, I knew it was a much bigger job than the one I had and could put me on a different trajectory. On the other hand, the job was mostly a financial one and I had never had a financial job in my life. Sure, I knew how to read an income statement, but to run the finance department seemed daunting. I took the job, which laid the foundation for my later promotion to president.

What I realized was that, from time to time, you have to get out of your comfort zone. This is absolutely critical if you stay in one organization for a while. You must avoid complacency and getting too cozy in one spot. You have to continue to challenge yourself and put yourself in uncomfortable assignments. That's how you'll learn and continue to grow as a professional.

I feel very lucky that the first and only company that I've ever worked for was the kind of company where I could build a career. It's when you find a place like that that I suggest you hold on for a while. Most of us will work for three, four, or even five decades. If you switch jobs and companies every year, then you're going to quickly run out of places to work. What you do early in your career often sets the tone for the rest of it, which is why I hope people in their twenties have a chance to work in an organization that inspires them to stay in it.

23

Unplug — and Tune In

Even though Paramount Pictures executive Amy Powell has risen to the top of the hard-charging world of Hollywood, she underscores the value of staying grounded and maintaining a balanced life.

by Amy Powell

As senior vice president of interactive marketing for Paramount Studios, Amy Powell brings over ten years of marketing experience in the entertainment industry. She has created, developed, and executed integrated marketing campaigns for films including *Transformers*, *Iron Man*, *Indiana Jones*, *Spider-Man*, *Mission Impossible*, and *War of the Worlds*.

I spent the majority of my twenties plugged in to some form of technology at all times, always rushing both physically and mentally to find my next challenge in life. When I turned thirty, a series of significant events forced me to realize the importance of slowing down, unplugging, unwinding, and enjoying the here and now.

I'll admit, slowing down hasn't been easy for me. I'm a total Type A personality. A taskmaster, a planner, a have-to-get-it-done-yesterday overachiever. As a child, I was in a rush to do everything: to walk, talk, and ride my bike. I was first in line at the ice-cream truck and the last child to drift off at a sleepover. My kindergarten teacher was exasperated by my refusal to take naps. But I couldn't fathom why all the other kids were so tired! It was only 10:30 in the morning. Didn't we just wake up?

As I grew up, my go, go, go mentality only increased, along with the pace of technology. Along came cell phones, e-mails, high-speed computers, BlackBerries — amazing innovations that would allow me to do MORE in LESS time! There was no shortage of things for me to do: learn yoga, master cooking, travel the world, renovate the house, volunteer, and fundraise. I spent months on end rising at the crack of dawn, succumbing to sleep only when my eyes refused to remain open any longer. I was always rushing somewhere. I was young, I was healthy, and I was living the life of my dreams — full to the brim. I felt infallible! Until the spring of 2007, when unscheduled and unplanned, my life changed.

It was a hot New York City day and my husband and I were off to meet his parents for brunch. As we walked down 57th Street, I was hit with an excruciating pain in my right hip. I literally couldn't lift my right leg. Of course, my three inch high heels probably weren't helping, but regardless of that, I could hardly walk. After proclaiming that I was fine, I hobbled into brunch. My father-in-law, a doctor, found my pain peculiar and insisted that I have my leg X-rayed upon my return to Los Angeles.

After multiple tests and meetings with various orthopedic surgeons, I had a diagnosis: a stress fracture in my femur. I immediately thought about spending my summer on crutches. As a kid, the notion of being on crutches was heavenly: loads of attention and sympathy, how fabulous! But as a thirty-year-old woman who relished speed and agility, this news was devastating.

After all, I had a long-planned trip to France. I had visions of sipping champagne on the Croisette, winning craps in Monte Carlo, and lounging on the beach in St. Tropez, not sightseeing on crutches. I had spent weeks researching every restaurant, shop, and café. We were going and no one or nothing could stop us, and by "us" I meant "me."

After a brief connection in London's Heathrow airport, where I declined a wheelchair; insisting on crutching the ENTIRE excruciating twenty-minute walk to our connecting terminal, we were finally in Cannes! It was full of gorgeous people, sweeping white sand, and crashing blue waves, and it was 100 degrees. My leg was throbbing and my triceps were burning, but I refused to let the crutches stop me.

My carefully planned itinerary called for a day trip to a lovely hill-town village.

I was doing well until we approached the destination and discovered that this "hill-town village" was LITERALLY built into a hill. But true-to-form, I was up for the challenge. I got out my crutches and began making my way up the hill to enjoy a "fancy" French meal.

As we made our way up the insanely steep hill, one

of my crutches came out from under me and I slipped and fell. HARD. And as if that weren't bad enough, my crutch went tumbling down the hill, bouncing off several tourists along the way. I lay on the cobblestone street in my freshly pressed white sundress, a crumpled mess. I was trying to decide if I should laugh or cry. Then, all of a sudden, I began laughing hysterically. Laughing so hard my shoulders were shaking and tears were streaming down my face.

The wipeout was clearly a sign that I needed to slow down.

I never made it to my fancy French restaurant; instead I had a slice of the most delicious pizza I've ever tasted. Right there on the curb, dirty white sundress and all. And when I got back to the hotel, I slept for a whopping eighteen hours.

And so the vacation ended and I returned to my firing-on-all-cylinders life in Los Angeles. Only, a little something had shifted inside me. My sojourn from my wired world had given me a deeper appreciation for the necessity of slowing down.

The advice here: Unplug. Ditch the BlackBerry. Turn off the cell phone. Power down the computer and slow down. Connect with the people in your life, not just the technology in your hand. Sit and talk with someone, gasp, in person. Or yes, take a nap. That e-mail, text message and to-do list will be there when you wake up. Nothing is so important that it has to be tended to immediately, except you.

Slow Down and Focus Inward

A well-known feminist activist writes of her decision to have a baby and all that goes into making this life-changing choice.

by Amy Richards

Amy Richards is the author of *Opting In: Having A Child Without Losing Yourself* as well as the co-author of the widely acclaimed *Manifesta: Young Women, Feminism and the Future*. In 1992 Amy cofounded the Third Wave Foundation and in 1995 she created her still popular "Ask Amy" online advice column.

My twenties were pretty much all about me — my biggest daily obstacle might have been getting out of bed by 9:00 a.m. I traveled the world (Cuba, Ghana, Egypt), tried the unexpected (whitewater rafting in Zimbabwe), and otherwise treated myself to things I simply felt entitled to (an Armani suit for one). To be fair, these indulgences were mostly "rewards" for the many sleepless nights I had trying to create the Third Wave Foundation, a small nonprofit organization for young feminist activists, and my other tireless efforts to "save the world." In fact, many of the late nights and social events were professional and political at their root: I was trying to spread awareness and raise money to sustain the work I cared so deeply about.

As I inched toward thirty my life started to change, really everyone around me started to change. Most friends were getting married, buying houses, getting graduate degrees, building up their 401(k)s, and ... having babies.

By the time I turned thirty, I, too, started seriously contemplating having a baby. The high-profile "news" that age might limit my fertility was also an *unhelpful* reminder that I was getting "old." A long time boy-friend dumping me because I didn't make him my top priority was equally sobering: if I wanted a home life it was time to plan accordingly. But really I was ready for this change and convinced that my twenties were to my professional life what my thirties should be to my personal life. It was time to scale back, slow down, and focus inward. To wit, I threw myself a fancy thirtieth birthday party for thirty friends — exotic cocktails, a sit-down dinner, loads of fun and merriment; a farewell to my carefree twenties and a hello to adulthood and adult things.

As luck would have it, early in my thirties I fell in love with someone and shortly into our relationship, I learned that he was ready for kids, too. Within a few years we had our first child and two years later, our second. Though I always preferred the idea of having a baby with someone I loved, I was also willing to skip marriage and never felt that I "needed" a traditional family. I simply wanted to become a mother and I wasn't scared of having a kid on my own — a confidence I certainly got from my own unconventional upbringing: I was raised by a single mother and never knew my father, and one of my closest family friends adopted two children from Korea when I was still very young. With these very personal and early examples, I knew that motherhood was accessible even if I wasn't married or fertile.

Of course my transition from single and social to domestic and doting didn't happen overnight, nor were the differences in lifestyle really that stark: though now I do prefer going out to dinner at 6:00 p.m. rather than 8:00 p.m., and I do get embarrassed by how much more I know about *Curious George* than world news. This "turning point" is also a perspective I couldn't have offered in the moment. Only by reflecting back over my life can I identify how deliberate some of my choices were. Or perhaps it's only in hindsight that I can acknowledge how much I wanted a change. And while I have always recognized that having kids would be a defining moment in my life, I would also never presume that others must have babies or need kids to feel complete.

As my kids are growing and I feel increasingly more "forty" than "thirty," I actually think I made my choices in the right order, spending my twenties defining who I am as a person and my thirties more focused on family. In my twenties, I discerned my likes and dislikes, I worked through any residual baggage of my childhood, secured my life-long friendships, analyzed my political beliefs, developed a hobby, and figured out my value system, what motivates me, and what I care about. That's precisely what our twenties are about — it's the first time most of us are given the freedom to explore life on our own and try things that perhaps our parents shunned. It's also the first time that most of us have to be accountable beyond ourselves, without the automatic safety net of our families. We use this time precisely to embrace what we always loved and reject what always felt forced.

All of the questioning, challenging, and confidence-building I did in my twenties made me a more secure person and thus better positioned to embrace parenthood. I was less conflicted about what I was "giving up" or "losing out on" because I had already established myself as a unique individual. Likewise, I was invested in myself enough so I wouldn't fall into a dangerous position of letting my children's lives overtake my own. Had I not developed a strong sense of self, I might have been more righteous about having to accommodate my children's schedules at the expense of my own. Had I not had time to myself, I might have been more hesitant to relinquish some of my "me" time.

And yet, I was also won over by parenting in a way I hadn't expected — I actually do enjoy spending hours reading with my kids or playing hide-and-seek for the umpteenth time. I love having quiet nights at home with "just the family," as my four-year-old son says. And I do prefer just spending time together — taking a walk across the bridge, going for a bike ride, spending fifteen minutes looking at the clouds in the sky. But I'm not sure I would have been able to take as much pleasure in my parenting had I not first prioritized "me."

Had I had children in my twenties I might have had a twinge of resentment. I might have felt they were robbing me of the experience of traveling to exotic places, having some disposable income, and unconditionally supporting my friends. Or I would have put too much pressure on my children to help me fulfill my expectations. I would have lived through them — an unrealistic goal and an unfair burden on them.

If I had waited much longer to have kids I might have become too set in my ways and thus would have been more stubborn about succumbing to the inevitable compromise that comes with children. Or at the other extreme, I might have felt extra-precious about my children and therefore would have been more likely to cave to their perceived needs rather than focus on any of my own needs. I might also have been too aware of how short our time together might be.

All those years ago, this is the exact conundrum that feminism warned women about — how to have children, something most of us want, without having to do so while also adhering to a limited role that society has scripted for mothers. But as my example attests, what is possible for this generation of women is that we can be ourselves first and mothers second. We no longer are expected only to find ourselves and our purpose through motherhood or funnel our ambitions through our children.

As I look toward forty, I am looking to return to that passion and those long nights that I had in my twenties. And while I in no way took a break in my thirties — I did step onto a different track, which only revitalized me. I can continue that journey now, not only because I love the work but because of whom I love. As much as I want to work purely for myself, my children need that example to inspire them about what is possible.

Section

STRETCH YOUR HORIZONS

25

Enter the Dragon

Sexpert extraordinaire, the author reveals why thirty is an age to explore, push the envelope, and tap your pioneering spirit.

by Susie Bright

Susie Bright is the co-founder of the first women's sex magazine, *On Our Backs*. She founded the first women's erotica book series, *Herotica* and was the editor of the highly acclaimed *Best American Erotica* series. Bright is a popular speaker and she has taught at the University of California, Santa Cruz. Susie Bright's Journal can be found at susiebright.blogs.com.

No One Can Trust You: Finally!

This is your decade to confound and surprise everyone. Neither your parents nor your peers are your masters any more — you hold them all with a healthy skepticism (and appreciation).

The famous sixties counterculture slogan "Don't Trust Anyone Over Thirty" — was taken to mean, in its time, that old people were sell-outs, capitulators, snoozers. But when you turn thirty today, you realize the true value of that quote is the realization that, after thirty, you cease to be predictable. You stop selling out to peer pressure; you suspend the reactionary tete-a-tete with your relatives. You're the one to initiate now. You're making your own moves, and those lines are going to be etched on your face, not theirs.

At thirty, you're capable of sacrifice, of acting with wisdom and foresight, on a scale that couldn't have been penetrated before. Instead of playing "truth or dare," you're dancing the dialectic, you hold risk and caution in both hands. Your candor is tempered by prudence and ginned up with playful dark humor. Thirtysomethings have the capacity to change everything, not just to startle or elbow. Revolution has offered its personally engraved invitation to you: Go For It.

Burn the Candle at Both Ends

Light it up, from every standing wick. The thirties are the only decade you can pull it off. Go ahead, wear yourself out! Take on too much; blow your wad. This is your moment of peak physical capacity — in terms of endurance — and it's also the first time you have the developmental chops to handle hindsight, foresight, and unspeakable stress in the same cosmic moment.

When you were younger, you might've been able to run faster, but you didn't know where the fuck you were going. When you get older, your knees will give out. The sweet spot, the thirties, is where you can still look like a million bucks, but you've found out that "pretty" ain't the only card in the deck. Thirty is when you can think on your feet and sprint at the same time.

Sleep deprivation? This is your decade for it. Two jobs, three lovers, and four dependents? You can pull it off for this limited time only! "Dance all night and grind all day" is your mantra for the thirties. On the other side of it, your elders will pluck out your first gray hairs.

Have a Baby

Go ahead, have two. You've had a good run of thinking of nothing but yourself — whether you were the Golden Child, or the Bad Seed, or Brimming with Potential. Give someone else a turn . . . or rather, discover the heroic journey of parenthood. To be the Nurturer will change your sense of life's possibilities more than anything you've ever tried. There's no intrinsically bad time to raise a child . . . there are great parents who are teenagers as well as those who are embarking on this journey in middle age. But the thirties not only offer fresh female eggs, they also give you the physical capacity to cope with a colicky infant — no laughing matter — and also the emotional strength, that you'll need when you're in your forties to deal with the brain-fry of adolescence. You'll require every advantage, and at thirtysomething, it seems like a unique moment where you're neither too young for anyone to say you don't know what you're doing, nor too old for neighbors to call in the cavalry to assist you in the changing room.

You will never love anyone like the children you raise. Not your parents, not your soulmate. You go in deep with kids, and their little fingers make sticky marks on you, where no one else could ever reach. You'll make a complete fool of yourself, unleash tyrannical rages, sob awestruck at their beauty. For them, the babies, it's just another day with Mom and Dad, Auntie and Uncle. The sight of their eyes, those dark little pools, peering into yours for an answer — for your love and protection — will bring you to your knees. Bring lots of padding.

Think of What Your Folks Were Doing at this Age

My parents got on a freighter in the late 1950s, and moved to India, not knowing a soul. They arrived looking like Dr. Livingston and Little Nell, complete with pith helmets — and they left with my mother in saris, and my dad sporting a beard he never shaved off again. They arrived in Bangalore as young marrieds, inexperienced and shy about sex, scared about how to make a living, uncertain about the future of their chosen field, linguistics — which, at the time, was a word most Americans couldn't pronounce. They had no idea what was going to happen to them.

But in her seventies, as she lay dying, my mom smiled at old snapshots of herself posing in her red sari, and told me those early thirties were the happiest years of her life. My dad was just out of the army, and thrilled to be doing something he really cared about.

Everything was about to change, the counterculture was on its beatnik cusp, and they blew out their thirty candles right in the middle of it.

Treat being thirtysomething as a generational sea change. Something remarkable is about to happen, and you have the front-row seat. You are going to be an actor this time, not a follower. You'll hold the beads in your hand, you'll count them, break a few, roll them around in your mouth. It tastes good to be in charge this time. All these years you've heard about "being just ripe," well now you know what it looks like: thirty firecrackers going off, thirty sweet plums giving up their flesh, thirty arrows seeking target. You can be trusted alright, to be absolutely unstoppable.

26

Be an Open Book

This basketball phenom says it's not just looking inward that enriches your life, but looking outward to the wisdom of others.

by Richard Jefferson

A seven-year NBA veteran, 6'7" forward Richard Jefferson was a centerpiece of the New Jersey Nets, becoming the team's all-time second leading scorer and is now with the Milwaukee Bucks. He has been a member of the USA's elite Olympic basketball "Dream Team," and most recently finished in the top ten in the league in scoring.

I should start out by saying that even though I'm twenty-seven years old, I never once thought about what someone should do when they turn thirty — or even before they hit that milestone — until I was presented with this chance to write about it.

Looking at my life so far, I feel I have been extremely

blessed and fortunate to have been given the talents and opportunities that I possess. I often have been asked, what would I be doing if I wasn't playing in the NBA? My answer is the same every time: "I never thought about doing anything else." This brings me to what I think is the most important thing a person should do before they turn thirty, which is to accomplish a dream or goal they have always had. Achieving a dream, no matter how big or small it may be, gives you hope, direction, guidance, and often times it can even give your life a sense of purpose. And to me, that is a critical component in living a fulfilled life.

It was hard work achieving my goals, but with each accomplishment I took comfort and solace in the fact that I was able to grasp a dream and turn it into a reality. I was lucky — I had the help of people who believed in me all along the way and they taught me to believe in myself as much as they did. It was that support of family, friends, and fans that helped me to realize that one of the most profoundly important things in life is connecting to other people, seeing the world through their eyes. Wherever I've been — whether it was growing up on the West Coast (or to some of you out there, the left coast), or traveling to Africa, or living in New York City, one of the greatest cities in the world — I feel that if I've learned anything in my life, it's to be open-minded, to try new things, to listen to what people have to say, to listen to the very people that others tend to neglect. I've always found that they're the ones who have some pretty amazing things to say.

Since being on my own, I've had an opportunity to visit a lot of different cities and meet new people everywhere. As my world gets wider, I've learned that the most valuable thing I can do is to discover who my true friends are. If you can find a good circle of friends, that (like the MasterCard commercial says) is "PRICELESS." I believe everyone should try and have at least one good friend by the time they turn thirty.

Basketball now takes me away from that circle some-times as I travel the world.

With each new person I meet, I feel that there's so much I can learn. We should all be fortunate enough to share our infinite wisdom with one another. The only way a person can expand their inner horizons is to listen and learn from other people. If we all took the time to listen to each other a little more, instead of talking all the time about what we, ourselves, feel is important — and believe me, I am just as guilty as the next person of doing this — then we'd be able to be exposed to so many new and interesting ideas, thoughts, and adventures. My final piece of advice about what to do when you turn thirty is this: be an open book, let the world and the people you come across fill the pages of your life book with their thoughts, their ideas, their infinite wisdom. Don't just flip through those pages, but take some time to really read them, to make sense of them, and most importantly, to put the ideas and thoughts of others to use in your life.

27

Go on an Outward Bound Trip

Fans worship her as a singer-songwriter, who's sold millions of records, but KT Tunstall writes about how an Outward Bound course taught her about nature and her own inward spirit as well.

by KT Tunstall

Kate "KT" Tunstall is an award-winning Scottish singer and songwriter, with massive hits like "Suddenly I See" and "Black Horse and the Cherry Tree." She's sold over four million albums, been labeled a "folk-rock goddess" by *Rolling Stone* magazine, and won three BRIT awards and two Grammy nominations.

The older you are when you go on an Outward Bound trip, the more humiliating the experience can be. But I did this in the spring of a twenty-something year, along with my younger brother, and I'll always be glad I did. I recommend everybody tries it at least once before they reach thirty.

It was actually my Dad's idea. My parents are big-time outdoorists; they met as mountaineers, and still walk for miles across the face of Britain at any given opportunity. It's a pastime I've come to love as I've grown up. But the Outward Bound course was a whole different kettle of fish.

I don't usually eat breakfast. I don't usually get up at 7:00 a.m. and jump in a lake with all my clothes on. I don't usually climb twenty-five-foot telegraph poles the diameter of a dinner plate, and fling myself off them to catch a trapeze hanging in mid-air. By the third day I was eating a huge plate of cooked food every morning, after the shocking thrill of spring water finding every pore at first light.

There are a number of challenges you face on an Outward Bound course. I vividly remember one task in particular: we had a pretend budget, and we had to design, 'pay' for, and build a raft to take twelve people across a lake. We had to do this as a group, and decide on a piece of paper what we were going to use (plastic barrels, logs, rope, paddles, you know the score) and how we were going to make the whole thing strong enough to ferry twelve people.

I was chosen to be group leader. It was then that I I realized how bossy I could be, how I don't listen enough, and how dreadful I am at interrupting people. We're not talking full-swing fascist raft-building dictatorship here, but I had thought I was laid back. Ho ho.

We did end up building a wicked raft, I'll have you know. But when we were losing the race across the lake against the other team, I remember hollering profanities at my brother, along the lines of "Please, will you paddle quicker!" He laughed at me, and I laughed back, but I was definitely sweating a little.

As by far the oldest member of the group, I had another unexpected role thrust upon me: giving advice to teenagers throughout the week about how to solve the sexual tensions caused by various other members of the group. But I didn't mind this bit of agony aunt duty, especially as the teens' soap opera was unfolding with convenient proximity.

I should point out that I was an unemployed busker at this point, not a singer on television. It was nice to be asked, and I realized I had a few answers under my belt.

Sitting in the morning sunshine up a mountain with a view of snowcapped hilltops, miles from the main house after lugging a huge backpack and pitching a tent in a horizontal blizzard the night before, I felt my age: young! Also, really tired, and really happy.

I made tea on my stove for our group, and ate a meal out of a bag. I loved sleeping in the tent with my little brother, the wind whipping at its sides all night. We laughed along with a bunch of nice people I would never have normally met, and drank in the simplicity.

It's easy for life to get complicated, especially as we grow older. Getting into the woods and the wilds, throwing myself over obstacle courses, getting really dirty, and pushing my body to its limits was seriously refreshing. I found perspective, and saw some extremes within my own personality — both good and bad. All in all, it was a mighty good way to spend a week. If you're just about to turn thirty, stretch your horizons — and immerse yourself in an Outward Bound trip. You'll discover the beauty of nature — and maybe even learn something about your own spirit as well.

28

Get on a Jet!

This Web entrepreneur, author, and world traveler recounts how seeing the globe is the perfect antidote for anything ailing the soul.

by Teresa Rodriguez Williamson

Teresa Rodriguez Williamson is a jet-setter extraordinaire. She created TangoDiva.com, a worldwide online social network and travel magazine for women. Teresa authored *Fly Solo: The 50 Best Places on Earth for a Girl to Travel Alone*. Her dream was to connect and empower women around the globe with the inspiring wisdom she gleaned from her trips.

After three grueling weeks of daily therapy, my doctor apprehensively smiled as she handed me a three-pound stack of forms, "Teresa, I fear that our work together is not intensive enough. I recommend some time as an inpatient in our lovely facility near the rolling hills of San Francisco."

"What?!" I thought to myself. "I came here because I

was having issues with my husband who is divorcing me. Now this skinny, mouse-like doctor is about to send me to a psychiatric ward!" I suspiciously grabbed the stack from her hands, and she then handed me my Valium for the next few nights. She said that I didn't need to return to the hospital until the next Monday — the day I would go from a twentysomething to an inpatient in a psych ward.

As I stepped out from the stale hospital air, I asked myself, "How did I end up here?" I was merely trying to survive, while struggling to get through a divorce that was ripping at the seams of my heart. Holding the solemn stack of papers, which now carried the weight of my shattered life, I stopped in the parking lot and looked up. A band of black birds danced in the sky like velvet confetti, and the words from *One Flew Over the Cuckoo's Nest* rattled in my head: "One flew east, one flew west, and one flew over the cuckoo's nest." Looking up, I laughed at the sky and thanked the birds for their maniacal dance. Because it was at that moment, I decided that I was never going to return to that hospital to get my daily dose of Valium that lulled me to sleep every night.

No, I would follow the lead of the birds above me: Fly — jet — get the hell out of town before I slip on some very unflattering pastel hospital coordinates. I might be losing my mind, but I was not losing my fashion sense.

So jet is what I did.

I was supposed to be hospitalized the following Monday. But instead, I boarded a Pam Am flight to London wearing a darling outfit. "Hell, if I am going to go crazy, I'd rather do it in Europe with a glass of wine in my hand!" I jetted with a backpack filled with chic clothes, a wallet with a few hundred dollars in cash, and a heart brimming with hope. Little did I know that this first adventure was the start of my new life as a confident, international jet-setter.

What I find so astounding about traveling is my ability to leave the past behind and enter a new world that demands all of my attention. It is hard to get wrapped up in love gone wrong when I'm trying to cross the street in London, and it's even harder to worry about calling my lost love while trying to speak French with a young man in a Parisian café. When traveling, especially by yourself, you must give your attention to the present moment. In life, we tend to live in the past or in the future, and we let the delicious present slide through our fingers like pastry sugar. For me, my past was filled with rhetorical regrets. "What could I have done differently? Maybe he would love me more if I …"

My future, as well, was fraught with anxieties, "Where will I live? No one will love a twentysomething divorcée!" It was not until my time traveling alone that I learned the power of the present. Instead of spending hours grieving over my failed relationship, I'd take a train to Paris. When I felt the tickling need for friendship, I'd walk into a pub and talk with strangers. When the cold wind of loneliness would hit me, I would rush into a boutique and chat with the sales ladies. Through this odd form of coping, I gained an inner strength that I did not know I possessed. Frankly, I did not have time to cry over my spilled milk — I was in Harrods, drinking tea and eating biscuits.

During this time, I learned about my own strength, my personal ability to rise above my issues and start again. Plus, no one knew me in Europe; I could be anyone I wanted. They did not need to know that just a week before I was thinking about jumping off the Golden Gate Bridge, and that the only way I could fall asleep was with pills. What they did know was that I was a young, energetic woman from America who was taking the summer to walk through all the museums in London and taste her way through Paris. They knew that I loved pizza from a stand in Piccadilly Circus, and that I never ate escargots. Many learned that my favorite color was white, and that I thought Duran Duran was perfect. But none of them ever saw that miserable, weak girl who felt like she lost her life because she lost her husband. Funny enough, after a few nights away I, too, forgot about that girl. I haven't seen her since.

Through my solo travels I learned that I can make it on my own, that even if someone breaks my heart, they cannot break my soul. I learned that I can live off one meal a day. I know that I can talk to strangers and ask for directions. I know that no matter what happens to me, I will always have me. And I really like who I've become during my time jetting through Europe.

It is true that every day is the day that you can change your life. For some, it is hard to do that in the confines of their daily lives. If that's the case for you, treat yourself to a much-needed holiday. Jet! Go someplace where no one knows you, and reinvent yourself. Want to be a travel writer? Great. Want to be a happy, successful world traveler? Fabulous. You can, and nobody needs to know that you and your grandmother are the only ones who are going to read your travel stories.

So, back to those two beasts: worry and regret. I trust that you can relate, because it is so easy to get wrapped up in the drama of "all things but the present." While worry and regret don't go away with age, you can learn to tune them out and focus on yourself and the present. For me, the best way to gain that focus is to leave my emotional baggage at home and pack my physical bags and spend some time alone. You don't need to jet to another country to connect with yourself. Even taking the phone off the hook or driving to a nearby town can be all the "jetting" you need.

"Jetting" is about respecting yourself. During your "jet," make sure that you nurture yourself. Treat yourself like royalty and respect your needs. Like many others, you may spend so much of your time making others happy, you might find it difficult to let go of your need to please and instead, just be. That is the first step.

The next step is to be confident with your decisions. The way you do that is by giving yourself credit for all the amazing and wonderful things you have accomplished. Sure, somewhere between ages nineteen and thirty you'll make some really stupid decisions, but that's part of the fun. Ironically enough, you might not think that you made the right choices, but it is the set of choices you make that can ultimately lead you in the right direction. For example, if I did not mess up my first marriage, I would not have ever traveled alone, and I would not have become so successful in the travel industry.

While jetting, it's important to not take yourself too seriously. (As a matter of fact, don't ever take yourself too seriously.) Jetting, for me, was the perfect way to practice this lesson. When traveling, no one is paying much attention to anyone else. That is great news for you, because then you can try out a bunch of silly things you would never do with your co-workers: practice a new language, or sing folksongs with Icelanders. This is your chance — before you have kids, mortgages, spouses, and more responsibilities than you can pack in a carry-on. Go jet, have some fun, do something that scares you. Because if you don't, you might end up in a lovely facility in the rolling hills near San Francisco. And I can't think of anything scarier than that.

29

Conquer a Fear

In her year-long process of trying one new thing a day to usher in her thirtieth birthday, this author-editor discovered a way to take small, seemingly painless steps to conquer a much larger fear.

by Jen MacNeil

Jen MacNeil's (jen365, In the New blog) career history has included job titles such as entertainment editor, movie extra, bookseller, Blue Man Group tube talker, background singer, six-foot mouse, catalog writer (yeah, like Elaine on *Seinfeld*), copy editor, and author. She hopes to someday add mom, wife, and perhaps monkey trainer to the list.

I was, as many of us are, a fearful child. I had a mental list of horrors that would be at the back of my mind while I was brushing my teeth, slightly more vivid as I was climbing into bed, and then downright overpowering once the lights were out. But my fears weren't the typical childhood fantasia; I didn't fear monsters or boogie men, I feared fires and robbers. Perhaps I watched a bit too much evening news, or read the newspaper a little too closely over my parents' shoulders, but I somehow knew about these things and I knew they could happen to me. Even my mother's reassurances, night after night, that these things probably wouldn't happen to us, did little to assuage my panic. I somehow made it to adulthood, and over the course of the years the fears of robbers and fires gave way to a pervasive, if not crippling, fear of being judged by other people.

In high school, I was unpopular and geeky, more interested in theater and books than in boys or makeup. Beautiful and confident people terrified me. I worried that any wardrobe gaffe or uncool comment or strange personal choice would immediately become the subject of ridicule by anyone who took notice. For all of my teens and some of my twenties, I kept my mouth shut and tried to blend in.

One thing I never did fear was aging. As my thirtieth birthday approached, I watched many of my friends slip out of their twenties and into that dubious fourth decade. Some had small lists of goals they wanted to accomplish by the end of their twenties. Most didn't. I'd cobbled a small list together in my mid-twenties, and by twenty-eight had accomplished almost everything on it: I'd gotten a Master's degree, fallen in love, and moved to New York. Shortly before my twenty-ninth birthday, I thought about making a new list. I thought about big things I could do — skydive, get a tattoo, buy a luxury car. But none of that was really my style. I'd always relished the small accomplishments. Then it dawned on me — instead of going for a handful of huge things, why not do a ton of small things? Like one thing every day for the entire year before my thirtieth birthday?

So in the days leading up to the big 2-9, I started a list of the small things I would do by the time I turned the big 3-0. I e-mailed friends and started a blog online. The suggestions begin pouring in: "Write a love letter in pig Latin." "Use an old-fashioned washboard to wash your clothes." "Make a self-portrait out of food." After a few months, the blog got national attention from a major news outlet, and I began getting suggestions and letters of encouragement by the hundreds. What had begun as a fun idea turned into a year-long epic during which I would learn, do, seek, and experience more than any other year in my life. I would arrive at thirty having spent the year doing odd and exciting things that might otherwise never have occurred to me.

But at the back of my mind, what I really wanted was to go into my thirties with a sense of relief and balance. I wanted to get rid of the fears I'd hung onto throughout my life. That wasn't exactly something I could tick off on a list — how could I "learn another country's national anthem" one day and "stop being afraid of people judging me" the next? I couldn't do that, but I could put the fear into context.

By June, I was three months into my list when I bought a stick-on mustache and decided I would wear it during a night out. While a friend and I waited on the sidewalk in front of the restaurant for another to join us for dinner, and with my heart pounding in my ears, I pulled out the mustache and slapped it on my upper lip. I got stares. I got questions. I got bolstered. Especially (and maybe only) because I had my good friend by my side, I felt as if there were a shield around me, protecting me from any negative reactions to my very odd choice in makeup. With every raised eyebrow,

I raised my head a little bit higher. When other people made comments, my friends pretended that there was absolutely nothing out of the ordinary about my foux mustache. The dormant fear that wanted so badly to overtake my newfound confidence began to stir, and I had to fight it.

I wore the mustache for the rest of the evening, even on the subway home. Outside the presence of my friends, the fear crept back a little bit. I got some stares. The fear began to simmer. I heard a snicker. The fear started to boil, and at my train transfer, I ducked my head while exiting the train and ripped off the mustache. Still, I was proud of myself for having faced all that outside judgment for so long. I was only slightly irritated that I was nearly thirty, in the throes of a fantastic, life-changing year-long project, and still so scared of being judged. And at least I knew I was on to something. If I could keep my judgment-fear at bay for an hour, why not longer? So what if I'd caved and ripped the mustache off? At least I'd done it for a little while. I made a mental note that the next time I wore something weird in public, it had to be for at least twice as long.

A few months later, I wore pajamas to dinner and a comedy show with a different set of friends. This time, I had to arrive prepared, and there was nobody by my side at first while I stood outside a restaurant on a busy street, waiting for friends and wearing cotton pajamas. Again, the stares. I fought the fear, refusing to let it overtake me. When my friends arrived, they cheered and took pictures. Somehow, this time, the fear didn't surface again. Even as we walked from the restaurant to the theatre, and as I again took the subway home alone, I managed to stave off that oh-so-familiar fear. I couldn't even sense it. Part of my resolve came from knowing that this time I couldn't just rip off a mustache. I had nothing to change into, no way to hide my red-and-cream two-piece sleep set. It was either forge on or crumble. I forged on.

The fortitude carried over several times for the remainder of the project. When I wore an eye patch to a birthday party. When I walked around town in a fake Mohawk. When I faked a leg injury so I could commute home with a cane. Each time, when the fear started to emerge that someone, somewhere, for some reason would judge me, that new confident person I was starting to become told it to shut up. I learned to deflect the fears before they even surfaced, and to relish the feeling of standing out in a crowd. I got to experience something so new and incredible that even snickers from groups of imposing, beautiful people on the subway couldn't dampen my spirit. Best of all, I was going to glide into my thirties with a new sense of confidence. If I can wear a mustache on the subway without anything remotely terrible happening, I can do anything.

30

Climb to the Top of Angkor Wat

This hotel titan and quintessential New Yorker writes about how the most formative experience of his life came halfway around the world, deep in the jungles of Southeast Asia.

by Jason Pomeranc

New York-born Jason Pomeranc is an innovative hotelier, passionate businessman, and art collector. He joined his family's real estate development firm, the Pomeranc Group, in 1997 and has been the force behind 60 Thompson in Manhattan's SoHo neighborhood, the first in a collection of properties known as Thompson Hotels. Jason received his undergraduate degree in finance from New York University and a law degree from Cordoza Law School.

B eing a born and bred New Yorker, I've often felt that all I needed in this world existed on the island of Manhattan. That is not to say that places outside of New York haven't always fascinated me, but just not the typical jet-setting destinations, like L.A., Miami and St. Barts. They have their time and place, but I'm thinking of cities and regions and countries that are so far removed in both manner and circumstance that they make you rethink your life, whether you want to or not. The ones that inspired Bill Bryson and Allen Ginsberg; Yoko Ono and E.M. Forster; The Beatles and The Clash. The places that conjure up decades of history, cultures, movements, and thoughts that we've never considered. The places that change us. Calvino's Venice or Hemingway's Cuba. As you turn thirty, think of the far-away city that beckons you. For me, that place is Angkor Wat. Sometimes, in order to love and appreciate your immediate world, you have to leave it for a while.

Angkor Wat is a temple located in the Angkor region of Cambodia. Angkor Wat translates as 'The Pagoda of the City,' and its five towers symbolize the five peaks of the legendary Mount Sumeru. Once the capital of the ancient Khmer empire, Angkor is considered by many to be the greatest lost city. At its heyday, Angkor was a major industrial and intellectual center. It covered a vast territory, even greater than Rome. Comparisons have been made to modern New York City. After a Thai invasion infiltrated the empire in the fifteenth century, the capital city fell into ruin. The jungles that had once surrounded the city grew upwards and outwards and anywhere they could. Angkor, and its legendary temples, was forgotten, encapsulated beneath thick masses of leaves and branches.

The story of Angkor's rediscovery reads like a myth. In the mid-nineteenth century, malaria-ridden explorers chopped desperately away at the jungle in an effort to reach the buildings on the other side. Below them, instead of packed earth, they found the face of the late tweleth-century ruler of the Khmer empire, Jayavarman VII, whose image was carved over and over on the stone towers of Bayon, another temple in the region. Henri Mouhot, the French explorer credited with "discovering" Angkor, called the city "greater than anything of Greece or Rome." But to simplify Angkor to comparisons is to flatten the city, to write it off merely as a cosmopolitan capital lost and buried, whose memory floats easily through the stone steps and disappears into the sky.

There are two ways to see Angkor. One is to merely see its beauty. When the sunlight hits, birds and monkeys fly and swing haphazardly through the jungle canopy. The temple is colossal, much grander than it appears in pictures or even on film. In the deep of night, stars bounce off the expansive moat surrounding Angkor Wat, their reflections glittering in the water. It feels like a small miracle, and yet a great one at the same time. It's paradoxically inspiring; it evokes the same feeling you have when reading a great writer, as if you are reading something you realize you've always felt but never could formulate into concrete thoughts. Above the water, daunting stone towers, massive in both size and grace, give the temple a feeling of indestructibility — ironic because at its base, the towers are essentially crumbling. This is why there are two ways to see Angkor.

The other way is to see its history, and, with it, the inevitable histories of all cities, because that's what surrounds you when you have climbed to the top of Angkor Wat. It's not just the temple that is crumbling. Siem Reap, the town four miles south of Angkor, is going through a similar transformation. For decades, the militant Khmer Rouge was active in Cambodia, making it a dangerous destination for tourists. Siem Reap has its own stories as well; the famous photojournalist Dith Pran was born there.

The history which has flourished at Angkor Wat, concealed beneath the fallen structures, ruins, and the interlacing roots of the trees and flowers, creates an essence of nothingness. Time as I had come to know it in my fast-paced New York was intangible here; an entity that bypassed me as swiftly as a light breeze. However, the perspective of history is encapsulated when visiting the temple of Angkor Wat, a structure built upon spirituality. This concept of time is sobering. It inspires a feeling of irrelevance; that we, as individuals, are truly inconsequential in the scheme of things and the trials and tribulations of our everyday lives are insignificant. It was the tranquility, the beauty, and the spiritual and historical breadth of Angkor Wat that altered my perspective at this particular point in my life. No longer did I view my years ahead as daunting; instead, I saw the progression of time as a natural occurrence: eventually, all of us will become remnants on this earth. Thus, time is of the essence.

Currently, the area of Angkor is deemed safe and tourism is expanding exponentially. As a developer, it might seem odd that I find the onslaughts of ritzy hotels and restaurants plaguing. But there's a bigger issue here;

Angkor is devising its own destruction. The water and energy needed to sustain these new developments are causing river pollution, and the temples aren't sturdy enough to handle the amount of tourists who climb them every day. I've even heard that the famous Bayon temple, with its carved stone faces, is noticeably sinking into the ground. Its cracks are widening more every day. I find these negative changes devastating for Cambodia's modernization. Its transition from an ancient city, rich with history, into a developing nation, only speaks to its citizens' desire to persevere. Beneath the scars of victimization, poverty, and civil war, the resilient people of Cambodia survive. The challenges I faced upon entering adulthood, such as determining a career path, becoming financially independent, and building upon personal relationships, pales in comparison to what Cambodia has experienced. I have come to incorporate this spirit of perseverance as I grow personally and professionally.

An inherent optimism exists beneath the covered ruins of Angkor Wat. Despite the hidden layers of rubble and roots, a sense of belief, spirituality, and optimism somehow found me. Now, when I find myself walking quickly down a fast-paced New York City street, I reflect upon my enlightenment in Cambodia. I acknowledge that beyond the bustles of my tiny island, there exists a realm in which we are all, at our core, spiritual beings, despite the ongoing developments of our modern world and our busy lives.

About the Commissioning Editor

Chris Taylor is an award-winning journalist. Formerly senior writer with *SmartMoney*, and the *Wall Street Journal's* magazine, he has been published in the *Financial Times*, *Fortune*, *Money*, *Esquire*, *GQ*, *Best Life*, and more. He has won journalism prizes from the National Press Club, the Deadline Club, and the National Association of Real Estate Editors. His new book *A Pocketful of Wisdom* is now available from Sellers Publishing. A native of Vancouver, Canada, he lives in Brooklyn with his wife and son.

Credits: